PUBLISHED by PARABLES
Earthly Stories with a Heavenly Meaning

Pathways To The Past

Each volume stands alone as an Individual Book
Each volume stands together with others
to enhance the value of your collection

Build your Personal, Pastoral or Church Library
Pathways To The Past contains an ever-expanding list of
Christendom's most influential authors

Augustine of Hippo
Athanasius
E. M. Bounds
John Bunyan
Robert Lewis Darby
Brother Lawrence
Jessie Penn-Lewis
Bernard of Clairvaux
Andrew Murray
Watchman Nee
Arthur W. Pink
Thomas Watson
Hannah Whitall Smith
R. A. Torrey
A. W. Tozer
Jean-Pierre de Caussade
And many, many more.

The Holy Vessels and Furniture of the Tabernacle of Israel

By
H.W. Soltau

AUTHOR OF "AN EXPOSITION OF THE TABERNACLE; THE PRIESTLY GARMENTS AND THE PRIESTHOOD;" ETC

The Holy Vessels and Furniture of the Tabernacle of Israel
H.W. SOLTAU

Published By Parables
February, 2020.

All Rights Reserved. No part of this book may be reproduced or utilized in any form or by any means, electronic or mechanical, including photocopying, recording, or by any information storage and retrieval system, without permission in writing from the author.

    ISBN 978-1-951497-33-0
    Printed in the United States of America

Readers should be aware that Internet Web sites offered as citations and/or sources for further information may have been changed or disappeared between the time this was written and the time it is read.

The Holy Vessels and Furniture of the Tabernacle of Israel

By
H.W. SOLTAU

AUTHOR OF "AN EXPOSITION OF THE TABERNACLE; THE PRIESTLY GARMENTS AND THE PRIESTHOOD;" ETC

The Holy Vessels and Furniture of the Tabernacle of Israel

CONTENTS.

    THE ARK AND MERCY-SEAT.   9

    The Throne of Grace

    THE TABLE OF SHEWBREAD   49

    The Dimensions of the Table .
    The Bread on the Table .
    The Frankincense . ...
    The Sabbath .
    The Crowns and Border

    The Vessels attached to the Table of Shewbread
    The Dishes
    The Spoons
    The Bowls and Cups

    THE CANDLESTICK   79

    The Shaft and its Branch
    The Bowls like Almonds .
    The Knops .

    The Flowers ....
    The Oil for the Light ....
    The Purpose of the Light .
    Time of Lighting and Dressing the Lamps

    The Vessels attached to the Candlestick
    The Tongs
    The Snuff-Dishes or Censers

THE ALTAR OF INCENSE   103
The Materials of the Altar.
The Dimensions of the Altar
The Horns of the Altar
The Crown and Staves.
The Tlace of the Altar
The Times of burning Incense.
The Incense

THE LAVER   123

The Foot
The Place of the Laver

THE ALTAR OF BURNT-OFFERING.   141

The Materials of the Altar
The Dimensions and Parts of the Altar

Vessels attached to the Altar

I. The Ark and Mercy-Seat

II. The Ark and Mercy-Seat partly covered; first with the vail, next a covering of badgers' skins, and over all a cloth wholly of blue. (Num. iv. 5, 6.)

III. The Table of Shewbread, with its attendant vessels; namely, spoons, or little vases, for holding incense, dishes for the bread when it was removed from the Table, flagons and bowls for drink-offerings. ,

IV. The Table of Shewbread partly covered; first a cloth of blue spread over it, with some of the attendant vessels placed thereon, next a cloth of scarlet, and lastly a covering of badgers' skins. (Num. iv. 7, 8.)

V. The Golden Candlestick, with its lamps; accompanied with the censers, tongs, and oil vessels. VI. The Golden Candlestick and vessels, partly covered with a cloth of blue, then placed within a covering of badgers' skins, and put on a bar. (Num. iv. 9, 10.)

H.W. Soltau

The Holy Vessels and Furniture of the Tabernacle of Israel

INTRODUCTION

The chief objects of the present Work are to give what is believed to be a more correct delineation, from Scripture, of the Tabernacle and its vessels, than has as yet appeared ; and to draw the attention of believers to a part of the word so eminently typical of the Lord Jesus, and which has hitherto been but little investigated, and feebly appreciated. The writer does not pretend to offer a full exposition of these types ; neither does he desire that his interpretation of them should be implicitly relied on, as it must needs be the true one : he is conscious of the vast depth of the subject, and of his own inability to grasp its extent : all he wishes is, to submit what he has written to the spiritual judgment of the saints of God, trusting there may be found in it that which shall, to some extent, interest or refresh ; and that there are not any fundamental errors touching the person or work of the blessed Lord ; though, doubtless, there may be mistakes as to the application of truth to the types sought to be illustrated.

The drawings of the vessels, contained in this first portion of the work, are executed on the scale of an inch to a cubit (except in the case of the Brazen Altar, the scale of which is half an inch to a cubit) ; they are the result of a careful and protracted investigation of the descriptions recorded in the Word of God It will be perceived at once, that they differ in many respects from all other plates of the holy vessels hitherto published ; this arises chiefly from their having been, as far as was possible, exclusively designed from the Scripture itself, — all Jewish tradition having been studiously avoided, and no pictorial representation that has hitherto appeared having been resorted to as authority. The absence of all ornament, and consequent simplicity and plainness, will at once strike the eye, in contrast with what has usually been represented. Where the definite shape of any of the vessels is not recorded in the word, but only their uses, as is the case with the

Laver, and minor instruments of service attached to the Shewbread table, Candlestick, and Brazen Altar, very ancient patterns have been adopted, in order that there might not be any glaring anachronisms in the designs. They are drawn partly covered as well as uncovered, as it is believed much of a typical import is intended to be conveyed in the various coverings directed to be used, in Num. iv. ; the illustration of which will be attempted in a subsequent portion of this work. The vessels are not drawn as arranged in their places in the Tabernacle, but as they may be supposed to have appeared when finished, and separately presented to Moses. (Ex. xxxix. 35-39.)

It may be asked by some, what definite authority there is for taking the Taber- nacle and its vessels for types. In reply to this, two passages in the Epistle to the Hebrews may be quoted, as distinctly affixing a typical meaning to all that Moses constructed at the command of God. Heb. viii. 1-5 : " Now of the things which we have spoken this is the sum : We have such an High Priest, who is set on the right hand of the throne of the Majesty in the heavens ; a minister of the sanctuary, and of the true tabernacle, which the Lord pitched, and not man. For every high priest is ordained to offer gifts and sacrifices: wherefore it is of necessity that this man have somewhat also to offer. For if He were on earth, He should not be a priest, seeing that there are priests that offer gifts according to the law : who serve unto the example and shadow of heavenly things, as Moses was admonished of God when he was about to make the tabernacle : for, See, saith He, that thou make all things according to the pattern shewed to thee in the mount. " And Heb. ix. 2 1-24: " Moreover he sprinkled with blood both the tabernacle, and all the vessels of the ministry. And almost all things are by the law purged with blood; and without shedding of blood is no remission. It was therefore necessary that the patterns of things in the heavens should be purified with these; but the heavenly things themselves with better sacrifices than these. For Christ is not entered into the holy places made with hands, which are the figures of the true; but into heaven itself, now to appear in' the presence of God for us." The first of these two quota- tions states, that the priests on earth "ministered an example and shadow of heavenly things; " and that God gave the express injunction to Moses, "See that thou make all things according to the pattern shewed to thee in the mount," when he was about to make the Tabernacle, because the type foreshadowed heavenly things. In the other passage we are told that the Tabernacle and vessels of the ministry were patterns of things in the heavens, and also that the holy places of the Tabernacle were figures of the true into which Christ has now entered. Thus, then, the service of the priests, the Tabernacle with its holy places, and the vessels of ministry, were respectively types of a service, places, and things in the heavens.

The order which is followed in the present work is one that results from that partly adopted in Scripture ; for three of the principal holy vessels are first de- scribed in Ex. xxv., before directions are given respecting the building in which they were to stand. The following pages will first treat of the typical import of the vessels ; should this portion of the work (which is complete in itself) be favour- ably received, the author hopes, with the Lord's blessing, to proceed with the Tabernacle, tracing out the minute details of its construction, together with the form of encampment : the dresses and ministrations of the priesthood will complete the third and concluding portion of the series.*

Previously to entering upon the subject immediately before us, it may be well briefly to point out three subdivisions into which the whole type of the Tabernacle is portioned out in the Word of God. Levi, the third son of Jacob, had himself three sons, Gershon, Kohath, and Merari (Num. iil 17); from these descended three distinct families of Levjtes, — Gershonites, Kohathites, and Merarites. They were numbered separately and encamped on a side of the Tabernacle definitely appropriated to each; to them also was assigned a distinct portion of the holy building as a charge and burthen. Thus the Merarites pitched their tents on the north, and to them was apportioned the charge, custody, and burthen of the boards, bars, pillars, and sockets : the Gershonites, who encamped west, had the charge of the curtains, hangings, and coverings : while to the Kohathites, whose position was on the south, belonged the care of the holy vessels. Here, therefore, we find three principal divisions of the subject The heavy foundations of silver and brass, and the massive frame-work of wood and gold, with the connecting bars and pillars, was a burthen appropriated to the Merarites : the charge of the beautiful embroidered curtains and hangings, with the other draperies and coverings, formed the Gershonite sphere of service and to the Kohathites was allotted the guardianship of the various vessels of ministry. Separate branches of truth seem to be typified under these three portions of the subject. All that solid foundation truth respecting the Lord Jesus, as God and man in one person, upon the right faith in whom depends the soul's appreciation of all other verities, is typified by the Merarite burthen : the whole superstructure de- pended upon the solid frame-work and foundations borne by them. The beautiful and costly curtains and hangings, which were the charge of the Gershonites, picture to us the beauty, grace, and holiness, which ever attract the eye of faith, displayed in the manifested character, ways, and words of the Lord Jesus — that " grace and truth " which was exhibited in all the varied development of His character here. While the holy vessels, borne by the Kohathites, are types of those offices of Christ, which He holds and exercises as our great High Priest — the one Mediator between God and men. Nature, character, office, are thus the subjects mainly embodied, as well as separately displayed, in this type of the Tabernacle.

In attempting to traverse such a wide and blessed field of truth, well may we exclaim, "And who is sufficient for these things!" May "the good Lord pardon " all that is faulty and defective, and by His Holy Spirit direct and assist the heart and understanding both of him who writes and those who read the following pages.
• 44 The Tabernacle and the Priesthood." London: Yapp and Hawkins; Morgan and Scott. resurrect- n's seed at it, and significant.ed. For manifested and death ex. 10-14.) sorrow, and pilgrimage. •16.) They never view of ict and >irit was i of the country jime and, e land, gh each *er mani- •lation to 1 be, God its joy, till it has by faith be great.

The Holy Vessels and Furniture of the Tabernacle of Israel

THE ARK AND MERCY SEAT.

THE first holy vessel described, and commanded by the Lord to be made, was the Ark, with its cover — the Mercy Seat It ranked the highest of all the vessels of the Tabernacle, was alone placed in the Holy of Holies, and was the one vessel with reference to which all the ministrations and ritual of the Tabernacle service were conducted. Before this vessel the holy perfume yielded its perpetual fragrance ; the incense altar was placed also with direct reference to it ; the blood of the sin-offering of atonements was annually sprinkled on it and before it ; and the costly vail was its covering. Indeed, without it all the other vessels of the Sanctuary, and all the service of the priests, would have been comparatively useless and powerless ; because it was over the Mercy Seat that Jehovah dwelt, and manifested His glory ; and all worship, and every act of devotion, must be conducted alone with reference to Him, and derives its blessing alone from the sanction and power of His presence.

It might have been expected that the Ark, being the most holy and important vessel of the Sanctuary, would have been described last in order, and would have been deposited last in the Tabernacle itself, after the court around had been reared up, and the other vessels had been arranged in their places. Such, however, is not the order of God. His way is to lead first and at once direct to the highest and holiest thing, and into the highest and holiest place. To make Himself known, and to bring into His own presence and glory, has ever been His purpose; and faith has ever had no lower object, has expected no lesser end. So, in the very earliest revelations of Himself, and in the very first promises, we find truths still of the most strengthening nature, and assurances of future blessings that are still before us. The very first promise in the garden given after the fall of man, namely, the bruising of the serpent's head by the seed of the woman, is that which contains, as in a nucleus, every subsequent blessing. Christ, as made of the woman, was there foretold. His mysterious conception was therein involved; for it was to be the woman's seed, and not the man's. His death — his subsequent triumph in resurrection — the spoiling of principalities and powers — the exaltation of the woman's seed above the highest created being — all this, and all that was dependent on it, and resulted from it — was, as in a bud, involved in that short and yet all -significant promise. And this very promise remains the last to be fully accomplished. For the final triumph of the seed of the woman over the serpent will not be manifested till the very close of all revealed dispensations, when at the last Satan and death and hades are finally, and forever, cast into the lake of fire. (Rev. xx. 10-14.) Again, we find the hope that sustained the early saints in their path of sorrow, and trial, and suffering, was that which still animates the Church of God in its pilgrimage. They looked for a heavenly city and a heavenly country. (Heb. xL 10-16.) They were heirs of the same promise with ourselves. And though, indeed, their view of that city that hath foundations was, as compared with ours, but indistinct and distant, and though many a glorious mystery now revealed to us by the Spirit was entirely unknown to them, yet they afford us bright examples of faith, and of the pilgrim and stranger character, resulting from their steadfast gaze upon that country which they sought, and for the sake of which they were content to leave home and kindred here, and to wander almost as strangers and sojourners in a strange land.

God has ever presented Himself as the object of faith ; and though each dispensation, as it has rolled on, has brought with it some fresh and clearer mani- festations of Him, and has added thus some further truth and fuller revelation to what has gone before ; yet from the first to the last it has been, and still will be, God alone who is the object on which the soul rests for its salvation, its peace, its joy. And whether as " the Almighty God," as " Jehovah/' or as " the Father," still it has been the same unchanged and eternal God, on whom the saints have ever by faith rested, and who has been ever their hope, their shield, and their exceeding great reward.

Thus it is in the directions given concerning the Tabernacle : The Ark and Mercy Seat — the throne of God's glory and power in the midst of Israel — is first described ; and we subsequently get directions for the making other dependent and subordinate vessels of ministry, and the courts of the Tabernacle itself in which they were to be placed It seems as if the Lord would lead at once to' the great object that was before Him, namely, to establish a place for Himself in the midst of His people; and where He might meet Israel's lawgiver and Israel's priest; and from whence He might give directions and commandments for their guidance and blessing. And all the laboured and varied services of the Tabernacle had for their end the preserving the people and the place of meeting clean, so that God might be able uninterruptedly thus to dwell among them* to* be their defense, their help, and their guide.

The Ark is thus described: — Exod. xxv. io, II. — And they shall make an Ark of shittim wood: two cubits and a half shall be the length thereof, and a cubit and a Exod. xxxvii. I, 2, — And Bezaleel made the Ark of shittim wood: two cubits and a half was the length of it, and a cubit and a half the breadth of it, and a cubit and a half the height of it. And he overlaid it with pure gold within- and without. half the breadth thereof, and a cubit and a half the height thereof. And thou shalt overlay it with pure gold; within and without shalt thou overlay it.

Thus the Ark 1 was a chest or coffer, as to its chief substance made of wood; the gold being its. casing within and without The Hebrew word in our translation called "shittim wood" is in the Septuagint always translated $v\ov fanprrov, "incor- ruptible wood." In seeking to understand this type, our thoughts will naturally be directed first to the materials of which this holy vessel was formed. The wood is generally, and I believe rightly, held to be a type of the Lord as to His human nature. Though truly man, yet in blessed contrast with all other men, the Lord was one whom neither the temptations of Satan could seduce, nor the evil around Him defile — one who, pure and spotless at His birth, withstood unmoved every (to us attractive) form of evil ; and though, like the shittim wood, planted and nurtured in this earth, yet abode uncorrupted and incorruptible in the midst of all the sin, defilement, and corruptions of man around, and attacks of the enemy with which He was assaulted. The shittim or incorruptible wood seems to be, therefore, a fitting emblem of that distinguishing characteristic of His humanity, its unstained spotlessness, its incorruptibility — that which nothing could taint or defile ; and yet, by reason of which, He is able to have MERCY SEAT. all sympathy and fellow-feeling for the weak and tempted, and to stand as then- fitting and glorious representative before God in heaven. It was needful that He who was to sustain the place of mediation between God and men should be able, on the one hand, truly to represent those for whom He thus stood, should thoroughly understand their need, should be able to feel for them and with them in their various temptations ; at the same time that He must also be fit for the most holy and glorious presence of God, must know and be acquainted with God as well as men, must be the " fellow " of God as well as of men (Zech. xiii. 7 ; Ps. xlv. 7) ; must Himself be asxompetent to be made the depositary of the thoughts and feelings and power of God, as of the need and weakness and wants of men ; and thus might be the channel of blessing from God to men, and the way of approach of men to God. The wood is then that material which shadows forth the nature of Christ as man, whereby He is able to take this place on behalf of men, for that He Himself truly is a man in glory ; whilst the gold which overlaid the wood within and without added its strength, its value, its brilliancy and glory to the wood, even so the blessed Lord, because He is Himself God, stands in His office of mediator in all His own divine and eternal power, glory, and preciousness, in the presence of God.

The use of the Ark was to contain the two tables of the Covenant, which were delivered to Moses at Sinai. " And thou shalt put into the Ark the testimony which I shall give thee." (Exod* xxv. i6> 21.). "And Moses took and put the testimony into the Ark." (Exod. xl. 20.) 2 The tables of stone thus put into the Ark, written on by the finger of God, were the expression of God's righteous demands of man, but they only ended in the ministration 1 of death. For the law found man a sinner by nature, and it had no power to alter that nature. It found him dead, and it could not give life. It pro- mised life indeed upon its terms being fulfilled, but it could not give life as a matter of grace. It declared the righteous requirements of God, both as regards what man ought to be towards Him, and also towards his neighbour. It declared what man ought to be, but it communicated no power to> enable him to be what it required. It demanded, and threatened, and denounced, but it could not give. It could condemn, but it could not save. It presupposed some power in man, but it found him im- potent. In short, the law, though an expression of what God demanded, was not God Himself ; neither did it manifest God in the grace of His heart : it did not describe God, so that it could neither communicate life — for God alone can do that — neither did it direct the soul to the source of life : all that it really effected was to sentence to death. " The commandment " was found by the apostle " to be unto death." (Rom. vii. 10.) Moreover, the law came in and interfered with the manifest actings of grace. It, as it were, stopped up for a while the wide outflowings of mercy. God had dealt with Abraham upon the sure ground of unconditional promise, therefore on the sure ground of grace; for unconditional promise and grace ever go together. Promise is the simple expression of God's own will and intentions, and its accomplishment rests alone upon God's own ability and unchangeableness : it requires, therefore, nothing on man's part God had also begun to deal with Israel upon the same gracious ground, up to their arrival at Mount Sinai " He smote also all the firstborn in their land, the chief of all their strength. He brought them forth also with silver and gold; and there was not one feeble person among their tribes. Egypt was glad when they departed; for the fear of them fell upon them. He spread a cloud for a covering, and fire to give light in the night. The people asked, and he brought quails, and satisfied them with the bread of heaven. He opened the rock, and the waters gushed out; they ran in the dry places like a river. For He remembered his holy promise^ and Abraham his servant." (Psalm cv. 36-42.)

God could thus deliver, and bless, and act in uninterrupted grace, though they from the first were a murmuring and stiff-necked people ; because they simply stood in dependence on Him, and He was dealing with them on the ground of His own promise. But now at Sinai all was changed; thrice had Israel, in their own ignorant self-confidence, uttered those fearful words, " All that the Lord hath said will we do, and be obedient." (Ex. xix. 8, xxiv. 3, 7.) And then Moses sprinkled both the book and all the people, and the covenant was confirmed, so that no one could disannul it ; a covenant which bound them to obedience, and bound God to punish dis- obedience ; a covenant that rested for the performance of its terms on their own faithfulness and strength ; and in which God had, so to speak, nothing to do Himself, but to watch the results of their actings, and to deal with them accordingly. And what were they? Poor lost sinners at their very birth, children of wrath by nature — without strength at the very outset, save that they had the strength of the flesh, which could only act in the way of sin. Doubtless, it sounded well in the ears of men when they uttered the resolution to obey God. It doubtless gratified their own hearts, and seemed like humble obedience; but what was it in reality but the expression of their own ignorance of God's righteousness, and of their own helpless and ruined condition. What was it but a proof that sin had so blinded their eyes that they were unable to discern their own state, and supposed themselves competent to obedience, when in reality they were in the helplessness of death. And does not many a good resolution, even at the present day, manifest the same ignorance of self — the same dream of strength when there is really none — the same thoughtlessness as to God's holiness and man's incompetence?

But though Israel proved themselves thus ignorant of their own lost condition, yet God, who searcheth the heart, knew it well ; and He commanded this golden depository to be formed, in order that it might shut up out of sight the very minis- tration of death, to which they had so eagerly and inconsiderately bound themselves. And thus, did He shadow forth the necessity of the law being removed out of the way, and point onward in this scene to Christ. It is blessed thus to trace in Scripture intimations, again and again, of God's thoughts, and purposes of mercy and grace, in the midst of the disclosures of man's folly, failure, and sin. It had been so before in Eden after the fall. There stood the woman who had given credit to Satan's lie ; had sinned against the majesty, and truth, and love of God ; had ruined Adam and the whole human race, and all creation besides, through her transgression ; but when to the eyes of all others she only exhibited a miserable spectacle of degradation, and ruin, and sin, to God she presented not only a fit object for mercy and grace, but the very one by means of whom He would affect His own most blessed joy and triumph. He spoke of her, not as the mother of the helpless and lost millions that were to spring from her, but as the mother of the seed that was to bruise the head of the enemy of God and man. He looked at the fallen woman, and He thought of Christ He saw His own joy, His own triumph over Satan, to be affected by the seed of the very woman who had so dishonoured, so wronged His majesty and love.

How quick, how skilfull, is love in discovering expedients to remedy the failure of those on whom it is set ! So was it at Sinai : there was Israel binding judgment and ruin upon themselves, exposing themselves willingly to all the righteous vengeance of God ; but God looked onward to one who would be able, and whose delight it would be to fulfil that very covenant on behalf of Israel, and who would thereby become the means and channel of blessing, mercy, and salvation from God to a lost and ruined world. There was, however, but one mode by means of which the law could be moved out of the way, and whereby also God's righteousness and truth could at the same time be preserved, and even vindicated; for the law was a fit expression of righteous- ness, such as God might justly demand of man. God could not lower this standard, and man had no power to attain to it Moreover, the covenant had been confirmed with blood, so that neither party could set it aside. It could not be disannulled or rent in twain, as a worthless thing; it was holy, just, and good; it was given by God Himself. There, therefore, it remained as the solemn witness of unapproachable righteousness in God, and of distance, and ruin, and helplessness in man. What, then, could be done? There was but one hope of deliverance, and the God of hope alone foreknew and foreordained, and in this type foreshadowed, that way of deliverance. Let one be found, a man made under the law, who should fulfil all its requirements ; who, placing himself in the sphere and circumstances of the guilty and impotent, should yet walk with unwavering perfectness along the prescribed path of strict, unerring righteousness ; who, amongst the disobedient, should prove himself obedient ; amongst the unholy, should prove himself spotless ; amongst the froward, should exhibit humble, patient dependence on God : one who should love when others hated ; should requite blessing for others' curses; should, in one word, "love the Lord his God with all his heart, and with all his soul, and with all his strength, and with all his mind, and his neighbour as himself." Let such an one be found, who should fulfil all righteousness, not only as to the letter, but spirit of the law. But even more than this was needed ; for Israel was not only impotent, and there- fore incompetent to accomplish human righteousness — Israel had done worse, for it had broken the law, and had incurred its fearful curse. Before the very tables of the testimony were brought down from God, Israel was found revelling in sin around the golden calf, and the law was broken at its very commencement ; sure and sad presage of what should afterwards be manifested by that law-bound people. Moses Seems to have felt the uselessness, as well as danger, of bringing the tables of the covenant into the camp ; and, hopeless as to the people, and but partially acquainted with God's resources in grace, he dashed the tables to pieces out of his hands at the bottom of the Mount. 3 The curse of the broken law had therefore to be borne, its vengeance had been incurred, and there was no provision of mercy, and indeed there could not be, in its requirements that could arrest its vengeance ; grace could not mingle with it ; so that judgment once incurred must find its path unobstructed, and must roll on unhindered and unarrested to its awful consummation. Someone had then to be found, who, while able to fulfil all righteousness, should also endure on behalf of others the deadly penalty incurred. And such was Christ, foreseen in the counsels of God, yea, foreordained before the foundation of the world, and in MERCY SEAT. the fulness of time sent forth by God, " made of a woman, made under the law, to redeem them that were under the law." (Gal. iv. 4, 5.) He " magnified the law and made it honourable." (Isa. xlii. 21.) He "is the end of the law for righteousness to everyone that believeth." (Rom. x. 4.) He has also borne the curse of the broken law; " Christ has redeemed us from the curse of the law, being made a curse for us; for it is written, Cursed is every one that hangeth on a tree." (Gal. iii. 13.)

The especial use of the Ark was then carefully to preserve the law, but to preserve it out of sight ; to remove it out of Israel's way, and for ever to conceal the ministration of death, and prevent its breaking forth in vengeance. A beautiful type of Him who, having come to do the will of God, and delighted in it, yea, even in His heart, having died also in accomplishment of that will under the curse, now stands before God as the one who has fulfilled all righteousness, and the witness also of vindicated justice ; and who has for ever removed the stern barrier that prevented matfs approach to God, namely, the demands against him of an unfulfilled law, so that now righteousness, which was the very hindrance, becomes the very ground of our full and free intercourse with God. Our way to God is not now by the law, but by Christ, by whom it has been taken out of the way and fulfilled ; God meets us in Him.

But not only was the testimony placed in the Ark, it was also covered up, and a sure provision made that it should no more be exposed. The Ark had a golden lid, of equal dimensions with itself, so as exactly to cover it ; and this lid was called the " Mercy Seat." Exod. xxxvii. 6-9. — And he mate the Mercy Seat of pure gold : two cubits and a half was the length thereof, and one cubit and a half the breadth thereof. And he made two cherubims of gold, beaten out of one piece made he them, on the two ends of the Mercy Seat ; one cherub on the end on this side, and another cherub on the other end on that side ; out of the Mercy Seat made he the cherubims on the two ends thereof. And the cherubims spread out their wings on high, and covered with their wings over the Mercy Seat, with their faces one to another ; even to the Mercy Seat-ward were the faces of the cherubims.

Exod. xxv. 17-21.— And thou shalt make a Mercy Seat of pure gold : two cubits and a half shall be the length thereof, and a cubit and a half the breadth thereof. And thou shalt make two cherubims of gold, of beaten work shalt thou make them, in the two ends of the Mercy Scat. And make one cherub on the one end, and the other cherub on the other end : even of the Mercy Seat shall ye make the cherubims on the two ends thereof. And the cherubims shall stretch forth their wings on high, covering the Mercy Seat with their wings, and their faces shall look one to another ; toward the Mercy Seat shall the faces of the cherubims be. And thou shalt put the Mercy Seat above upon the Ark ; and in the Ark thou shalt put the testi- mony that I shall give thee.

The Mercy Seat was thus the cover of the Ark, and both together formed one vessel of the sanctuary. We have to regard it, therefore, as a whole, and as such it typifies the Lord Jesus himself as the one mediator between God and men. For He, having fulfilled all righteousness, and having borne the curse of the law, and thereby having removed for ever the law, with its demands, and requirements, and penalties, out of the way, now stands in the presence of God as our way and place of approach to God ; and the one, also, because of and by means of whom God is able to be just, and yet the justifier of him that believeth; "the one Mediator between God and men, the man Christ Jesus" (i Tim. ii. 5), combining in Himself righteousness, mercy, and power, and standing in the mediate place, the means and channel of blessing from God to men, and the way of access from men to God. The first thing to be noticed respecting this Mercy Seat are the two Cherubim, beaten out of its two ends, one Cherub at the one end, and the other Cherub at the other end.

The Cherubim seem, throughout Scripture, to be symbolic figures, shadowing forth the glorious power of God, whereby He accomplishes His purposes by agencies often unseen, and yet sure, and efficient, and overruling. This power of Jehovah is first described minutely under these symbols in the book of Ezekiel ; where the Cherubim are represented as four living creatures, having every one four faces — the face of a man, of a lion, of an ox, and of an eagle.

The face of a man seems to be symbolic of mind, reason, intellect, knowledge, discernment, etc. And we can easily see how gracious a provision it is of God for us, that He who is our Mercy Seat holds and uses the power of God, guided by a full consciousness of all our need, of all our sorrows, of all our infirmities — having perfect human intelligence as to all these things, and able therefore so skilfully, and yet tenderly, to deal with us, and to accommodate this tremendous power, so that it may find its exercise in gentleness and grace.

The face of a lion denotes majesty, terribleness, strength, dignity; as it is written, " A Lion which is strongest amongst beasts, and turneth not away from any." (Prov. xxx. 30.) "The king's wrath is as the roaring of a lion." (Prov. xix. 12, xx. 2.) It is said of David, "And he also is valiant, whose heart is as the heart of a lion." (2 Sam. xvii. 10.) Lions were the emblems of the strength and dignity of Judah's throne (2 Chron. ix. 17-19); the name and title of its only true king — "the lion of the tribe of Judah." (Rev. v. 5.) And even for the maintenance of mercy, this power is needed; for who does not rejoice in Him who has proved His lion-like majesty and power, in the destruction of Satan and of death. And how needful is it that the same kind of power should still shelter and guard the place of mercy for us!

The face of an ox equally expresses power but used in patient and persevering labour; strength subjected to bear burdens. When spoken of with reference to God, it is expressive of long-suffering, or continued and patient exercise of power in subjection to love; " Much increase is by the strength of the ox" (Prov. xiv. 4); "able to bear burdens" (Psalm cxliv. 14, marginal reading); used to "tread out the corn." (Deut xxv. 4; Hos. x. 11.) See also the constant use of the bullock in sacrifice, as a type of the blessed Lord in His character of the patient, unwearied servant This characteristic of strength, thus connected with the Mercy Seat, is held by Him in the glory in order that mercy may still find its unrestrained exercise, in spite of all obstacles ; and may be steadily maintained, through the patient and enduring continuance of a power that will never weary nor be exhausted, but will still go on finding rich increase, and making fresh openings for the displays of grace.

The face of an eagle — marking quickness and power of sight, and almost equal rapidity of action. " She seeketh the prey, and her eyes behold afar off, and where the slain are there is she." (Job xxxix. 29, 30.) "Swifter than eagles," is used to express rapidity of action. How blessed to know that keenness of sight, and swiftness of execution, are attached also to the place of mercy; so that He who is the Mercy Seat discerns afar off, with eagle eye, the need, and quickly stretches out the hand of power to deliver.

These, then, are some of the attributes of the Cherubim, the executors of God's will; and here we find them beaten out of one piece with the Mercy Seat. Some have thought these figures betokened angels, and that their bending posture towards the Mercy Seat is explained by that text, " which things the angels desire to look into." (1 Peter i. 12.) And in many pictorial representations of the Mercy Seat we see them represented in a kneeling posture, as if in adoration. Others have thought that the Cherubim here symbolize the Church. But the construction itself, as well as uses, of the Mercy Seat seem to preclude either of these interpretations of the type. The Cherubim are distinctly stated to be " of the Mercy Seat," and " out of the Mercy Seat." (Exod. xxv. 19, xxxvii. 8.) And this is still more apparent in the Hebrew, where the preposition used in the 18th and 19th verses of ch. xxv., and the 7th and 8th verses of ch. xxxvii., and translated "on the Mercy Seat," and "on the two ends," etc, should properly be translated "from." Also, as to the word translated in Exod. xxv. 18, "beaten work," and Exod. xxxvii. 7, "beaten out of one piece," the meaning seems to be, that the Cherubim were not cast or moulded separately from the Mercy Seat, and then attached to it, but were beaten out of the solid mass of gold which formed the Mercy Seat, the one being beaten from out of the one end, and the other from the other. Angels cannot, then, be typified here by the Cherubim ; for, if they were, it would imply that they form part of the seat of God's mercy, and would thus stand very much in the place in which Popery has set them, as the agents for procuring or exhibiting the mercy of God, derogating thereby from the person and work of the Lord Jesus Himself, who is the only way of approach to God, and the one through whom alone God can show His grace and mercy to us; for "there is none other name under heaven given among men whereby we must be saved." (Acts iv. 12.) The same argument would equally apply, if the Church were symbolized by the Cherubim on the Mercy Seat The Church would thus become what, indeed, false systems have made it, the platform from whence God dispenses His grace, instead of the body which has received His grace. The Mercy Seat and Cherubim, being all of one piece, represents, it is believed, Christ as the one who holds all the glorious power of God, associated with mercy, and in and through whom God is able to display his power and righteousness, ever inseparably linked on with mercy and grace.

But the attitude of the Cherubim seems also to be significant " The Cherubim shall stretch forth their wings on high, covering the Mercy Seat with their wings, and their faces shall look one to another ; toward the Mercy Seat shall the faces of the Cherubim be." (Exod. xxv. 20, xxxvii. 9.)

When first seen on earth, the Cherubim were placed " at the east of the garden of Eden, to keep the way of the tree of life. v {Gen. iii. 24.) They then stood associated with " the flaming sword," the sword of vengeance and judgment ; and as witnesses that all the terrible majesty of God's power and holiness, which had been insulted, was against man, and had closed up every avenue against his return to his original happy state. The word and majesty of God had been trifled with and despised, man had given credit to Satan's falsehood, and had by his unbelief made God a liar ; and the Cherubim then took their stand as the avenger of God's insulted majesty, and the stern proof that man was an outcast, banished by God from that happy place, and no way allowed for his return to the tree of life. This significant place of the Cherubim of itself manifested the hopelessness of any attempt on the part of man to regain life by his own efforts ; and that, unless the glory of God could be met, and the flaming sword of vengeance and of holiness satisfied, it. were vain for man to hope for any way of return to life; but death* and the curse were his inalienable portion.

But to us the heaven has been opened, and there, in the holiest on the Mercy Seat, we behold these Cherubim of glory. The earthly garden, with its tree of life, is indeed lost, and lost forever, but " the paradise of God " is opened to us; and life above, hidden with Christ in God, is ours through faith in Him. The place of life and of the Cherubim is alike changed. They no longer stand to debar man's approach to life, but they brood with outstretched wings over the place of mercy, whence life and blessings flow. No longer are they connected with the flaming sword; but their faces now intently turn towards the place of grace. For all the power and glory of God is held by one in heaven, who uses it for mercy. " All power in heaven and earth " hath been given to Christ, but He now employs it but for one object, to preserve the place of mercy and of grace for His saints ; and the place where we now know the full propitiation for our sins, is the place where we beheld the majesty, power, and glory of God, all now in our favour, because forming part of the Mercy Seat itself. All the intelligence and sympathy expressed in the face of the man ; all the majesty, terribleness, and power of the lion ; all the patient endur- ing strength of the ox ; all the rapidity and clear-sightedness of the eagle, now stand engaged on the side of mercy. Redemption in Christ has converted the very attri- butes of God, which were once jthe most fearful and opposed to us as sinners, to be the very shelter for us, and the power, and assurance, and strength of our blessing.

Well, indeed, is it for the world itself that the faces of the Cherubim are thus turned towards the Mercy Seat, and that, for a while, He who holdeth this power hath retired into His place. For what will it be when again they turn their faces toward the earth? when again they look toward a world where not only the majesty, and glory, and truth of God have been despised, but where even His grace and mercy in Christ have been rejected? What will it be when the power and glory of God are made to test the condition of everything here below, and when Christ will come holding that power, and directing it against man in judgment? The day will ere long be, when "the Lion of the tribe of Judah" will rouse Himself to the prey, and, when riding on the Cherubim of glory, the Lord Himself shall return to avenge His own elect, and to destroy them that corrupt the earth. The Mercy Seat is only twice distinctly mentioned in the New Testament Once in I|eb. ix. 5, where it is enumerated with the other vessels of the Tabernacle; and in Rom. iii. 25, where it is in our version translated "propitiation," This passage in the Romans seems beautifully to allude to the type, and is another warrant for interpreting it as a type of Christ It begins by stating that, by the deeds of the law, no flesh shall be justified in the sight of God ; for that all the law could effect was to give the knowledge of sin, and not to put it away, or to give power over it. But now God's righteousness in justifying a sinner, independently of the law, has been made manifest, and is the portion of all them that believe in Jesus: a righteous- ness, indeed, to which the law and the prophets witnessed, though it was not then made manifest And in this respect there is no difference between Jew and Gentile — between one who has been seeking to keep the law and one who has not — for all have sinned, whether Jews or Gentiles, and have come short of the glory of God ; but all who believe are justified alike freely by God's grace, through the redemption that is in Christ Jesus, whom God had indeed foreordained, even before He came, to be a Mercy Seat, and, having Him in view, was able to pardon sins committed previously to this Mercy Seat being really established But now God has openly made manifest His righteousness in remitting sins, through faith in the blood of Christ ; for now God proves Himself just at the same time that He justifieth him that believeth. We are here instructed, in these great truths, the incapability of the deeds of the law to justify; the purpose of God to set up a Mercy Seat, even His own blessed Son ; and having that in His purpose, He pardoned the saints of old ; and now the Mercy Seat actually set up, and God's righteousness thereby vindicated and manifested when He pardons a sinner through Christ He receives the sinner now as "a just God and a Saviour." It is not> indeed, that Jesus turned the heart of God towards us, but that now God can act^ through Jesus, according to His own heart of grace and love, at the same time consistently with His righteousness and justice. For the law, the expression of God's just demands, has been vindicated, not a jot or tittle has passed away unfulfilled; its righteous vengeance also, on account of sin, has fallen on the head of Christ ; and now God can allow all His own full and eternal love to flow out towards the sinner, for justice has been satisfied, and mercy can rejoice against judgment In Christ, thus prefigured in the Ark and Mercy Seat, we can indeed say, " Justice and judgment are the establishment of thy throne ; mercy and truth shall go before thy face. Blessed is the people that know the joyful sound; they shall walk, O Lord, in the light of thy countenance." (Psalm lxxxix. 14, 15.) Here, " mercy and truth are met together, righteousness and peace have kissed each other." (Psalm lxxxv. 10.) Those principles which seemed to be most opposed to each other — mercy which desired to pardon, and truth which must condemn — meet together in Christ, for in Him the sinner receives pardon by the very means whereby the truth and holiness of God have been vindicated. And the apostle can therefore truly add, that "we establish the law" through faith, instead of making it void. We are not, indeed, saved by law deed; but our salvation is grounded on the fact, that the righteousness of the law has been vindicated and fulfilled. We establish it not as a means of salvation, not as attempting to save ourselves by fulfilling its demands, not as a covenant of works under which we are placed, but as that which has witnessed to and foreshadowed Christ, and the demands of which Christ has abundantly satisfied, both as to its requirements and its curse. And now no act more displays the righteousness of God than His act of mercy to a sinner; God never proves Himself more holy than when He pardons sin; for that mercy and pardon are ever grounded upon His righteous judgments having been poured out on the head of Christ, on behalf of, and as the substitute for, the sinner. God is "faithful and just" in the forgiveness of sins, and the very attributes of His holiness, which were most against us as sinners, become our surest defense and protection through Christ. The Cherubim of glory have quitted the flaming sword and taken their place on the Mercy Seat. But there are yet other parts of this holy vessel which demand our attention.

The Holy Vessels and Furniture of the Tabernacle of Israel

"And thou shalt make upon it (the Ark) a crown of gold round about" (Exod. xxv. 11, xxxvii. 2.) The word here translated "crown" occurs only in connection with the Ark, Shewbread Table, and Incense Altar. The Hebrew word it (zare) is translated by Gesenius, " border, edge, wreathed work:" he derives it from a root meaning " to bind together." This word has no reference then apparently to a regal crown, but means a ledge or binding of gold placed around the top of the Ark, the use of which seems to have been to retain the Mercy Seat in its proper place, exactly covering up the Ark.

The Ark had to be borne on the shoulders of the priests, over many a rugged path through the wilderness ; and they that bare it might even wander where their feet would be liable to slip or stumble ; many a rude shock would thus be given to this holy vessel ; and what if the Mercy Seat had been thereby displaced ? But this golden crown was the careful provision of God to avoid such a result, and to keep it securely in its proper place. Supposing the Mercy Seat had been displaced even accidentally, and not willfully, the law, the ministration of death, would have been exposed, and destruction to- the thousands of Israel might have been the result. We find one instance on record where this was done, not indeed through accident, for that had been carefully provided against, but from the unholy curiosity of those who lifted the Mercy Seat to look into the Ark. (i Sam. vl 19, 20.) "And he smote the men of Beth-shemesh because they had looked into the Ark of the Lord, even he smote of the people fifty thousand and threescore and ten men. And the people lamented, because the Lord had smitten many of the people with a great slaughter. And the men of Beth-shemesh said, who is able to stand before this holy Lord God? And to whom shall he go up from us?" May we not learn from this scene the awful consequences of the Mercy Seat being removed, though but for a little moment? Judgment necessarily then broke forth, and who could stand before the holy Lord God? If mercy is not fixedly retained by divine power covering over the righteous ministration of death, who indeed could stand?

The golden crown seems then to have been the gracious provision against this happening, notwithstanding the waywardness or stumbling of those who bore the Ark ; and the Mercy Seat was thus retained unshaken in its position, however the priests might fail or faint by the way. And so it is with the true Mercy Seat Not only has God, in his marvellous grace, appointed His Son to be His place of mercy, and our place of access and blessing, but He has provided that, through His divine strength and excellency, the ministration of condemnation shall be forever closed up, and kept out of sight. So that no wrath shall ever break forth against His people; no short- comings, no failures, no sins in them shall ever shake the stability of that throne of grace from whence all their blessings are dispensed. The place of mercy and of grace remains ever unshaken and unchanged for them. The ways of the Church of God have indeed been, in many respects, most evil ; declension, and backsliding, and failure to a fearful extent have marked their steps; as God's priests (Rev. i. 6), they have but little remembered the preciousness of the truth committed to their care, but have trodden many a bye-path of evil, and worldliness, and error. But still has the Mercy Seat been retained for them unshaken ; still no change has taken place in the position of Christ for them before God ; still has the way of access been the same ; still has the place of grace remained unaltered ; still does the same propitiatory abide ; and no intimation of wrath, no thought of anything but mercy is there in the mind of Him who has taken forever, as regards His Church, His seat between the Cherubim of glory over the Mercy Seat The thunders and lightnings of Sinai have been hushed forever, the law has been for ever taken out of the way, wrath has been appeased forever. " Mercy that endureth forever" seems to be the fitting motto for this golden circlet surrounding the Ark. Mercy that endureth for ever has been established on the ground of everlasting righteousness. And who has not felt the blessing of this divine power in Him who is our salvation, to retain unchanged his place before God for us, notwithstanding all our failures and haltings on the road? Who has not felt his need of casting himself, again and again, upon the unfailing ability of Christ to maintain his position before God for us, when we have wronged the grace, or trifled with the mercy and truth so richly bestowed? Who has not known the comfort of resting on one who, at the same time that He is plenteous in mercy, is also mighty to save?

THE STAVES.

Exod. xxv. 13-15. — And thou shalt make Exod. xxxvii. 4, 5. — And he made staves of staves of shittim wood, and overlay them with shittim wood, and overlaid them with gold, gold. And thou shalt put the staves into the And he put the staves into the rings by the sides rings by the sides of the Ark, that the Ark may of the Ark, to bear the Ark. be borne with them. The staves shall be in the rings of the Ark : they shall not be taken from it.

The fact of the staves being fixed in the rings, marked this vessel to be one that was to be borne with Israel during all their wilderness journey, and all their conflicts with the enemy. It showed that God intended all the value of this precious vessel to accompany them on their way, and to be ever present with them.

Israel had been redeemed out of Egypt, had been themselves saved from the wrath of God by the blood of the paschal lamb, and had seen God's judgments poured out upon their hard taskmasters, the Egyptians ; but the very redemption that had forever delivered them from the heavy bondage of those that oppressed them, placed them in a wilderness, where new scenes of trial, new sources of sorrow awaited them, and where a new class of dangers and enemies surrounded them. They had to learn, themselves, what their own heart of rebellion and unbelief really was and they had also to become acquainted with the holiness of that God who had delivered them, and who dwelt in their midst The Amalekites, Midianites, and Amorites, also, were enemies who would seek to impede their progress into the land of their rest ; and a trackless desert lay before them, where weariness, and toil, and hunger, and thirst, and a scorching sun awaited them. Under these circumstances, how gracious a provision were the staves thus attached to the Ark, which intimated to them that Jehovah Himself had foreseen their need, and had engaged to accompany them with His own presence all their journey through: one whom they might consult in every difficulty ; who would deliver them out of every danger ; who would be their defense and protection against all their foes; and in whom they would ever find sympathy, pity, and help, in all their distresses.

The Church of God is now going through an experience, of which Israel's history affords a type. The redemption that is in Christ Jesus has once and for ever freed the believer from all the vengeance due to him as a sinner. There is to him now no condemnation, he has passed from death to life : but still is he left in a world that is unredeemed ; still is he burthened with an unredeemed body, and present things around him are like the wilderness of old. His way is difficult, his path rugged. He has to learn his own weakness and worthlessness; he has to know himself. He finds desires, and thoughts, and feelings longing for God's presence and God's rest and holiness ; and yet he is in a world where all around speaks of vanity, and sin, and death, and where a groan goes up incessantly from all creation. He finds, too, a heart of unbelief and murmuring within, ceaseless in its efforts of evil, and active with a restless energy of sin, which it needs incessant watchfulness to restrain, and unceasing power to overcome. And there is, beside all this, Satan with his hosts of evil spirits hovering around the path, watching the weak points, suggesting occasions of evil, ready to take advantage of every failure, and marking with malicious exultation every declension. Ceaseless is the conflict, day by day is it renewed; day by day has a path of weariness, and toil, and danger, again to be trodden ; and still there seems before the eye to be further trackless wilds, stretching forth their long and dreary expanse, which have to be passed through ere the journey is over, ere the rest is entered. No marvel, then, if the heart sinks beneath it all, and trembles, and is discouraged, by reason of the length and difficulty of the way. And so it would be, were it not that there is the sure abiding presence of one, in all circumstances, who has said, "I will never leave thee, nor forsake thee;" one who has Himself trodden the path and has overcome, who has proved Himself fit and willing to guide, and guard, and comfort the hosts of the Lord on their journey. Is there failure? He is present to restore. Is there weakness? He is at hand to strengthen. Is there conflict? He is near to deliver. Is there ignorance? He is with us to guide. He who could say, " All power is given unto me in heaven and earth," hath also said, " Lo, I am with you always, even unto the end of the world." And as indeed redemption has brought us into conflicts, and dangers, and experiences, both of ourselves and things around us, quite different to what we once knew, and trying and sorrowful truly to the flesh ; yet we have one with us whose grace, and power, and holiness, could only be known in its full extent in such a scene as this ; and every fresh difficulty and temptation only proves an occasion for the manifesting of some fresh grace, and wisdom, and might in Him who, " having loved his own that were in the world, loved them to the end."

Israel might even have to turn back again, owing to their own sin and folly, and wander yet forty years in that waste howling wilderness, as a judgment on their rebellious hearts, and disbelief of God: but the Ark must turn back also; it could find no rest till they rested; the staves were still in the rings, and it must toil on still with that rebellious people ; for, though rebellious, they were yet God's people, and it must therefore still bear with them the wearisome journey. And think not, because there is failure, that the grace of Him who is our Ark and Mercy Seat has been exhausted. Think not His companionship is lost, think not His sympathy is lessened. With an anxious, careful eye still He marks the path of His saints ; though Himself in glory, and rest, and joy above, yet His heart and thoughts are here ; and never will He cease to watch over and accompany the Church below till He presents it to Himself a glorious Church, not having spot or wrinkle, or any such thing.

The usual place of the Ark during the journeying of the camp was, apparently, in the centre of Israel's hosts. For in Num. x. 13-28, where the order of their march is described, the arrangement was as follows: —
First : the camp of Judah, including under its standard the three tribes of Judah, Issachar, and Zebulun. Then the Gershonites and

Merarites, bearing the boards, sockets, and curtains of the Tabernacle. •

Second: the camp of Reuben, including under its standard the three tribes of Reuben, Simeon, and Gad. Then the Kohathites, bearing the Sanctuary.

Third: the camp of Ephraim, including under its standard the three tribes of Ephraim, Manasseh, and Benjamin. And

Fourth: the camp of Dan, including under its standard the three tribes of Dan, Asher, and Naphtali.

It will here be observed that the Kohathites march in the centre of Israel, having two camps of three tribes each in front, and two camps of three tribes each in the rear. They are said to bear the " Sanctuary," which word seems to mean here all the holy vessels, including the Ark. The word "Sanctuary" is used in Num. iv. 1 5 for the Ark itself. But at the end of Num. x. we find a remarkable exception to this order of march, as to the place of the Ark. 4< And they departed from the mount of the Lord three plays' journey, and the Ark of the covenant of the Lord went before them in the three days' journey, to search out a resting-place for them. And the cloud of the Lord was upon them by day, when they went out of the camp." The reason for this remarkable change of the Ark's position in the journey seems to have arisen from what precedes in the same chapter, relative to the conversation between Moses and Hobab.

The cloud is seen to rise off the Tabernacle of the Testimony (ver. 1 1) ; the priests encamped immediately in front of the Tabernacle mark this intimation of the Lord's intention to move, and sound, as directed in the same chapter, the silver trumpets, with an alarm for the camp of Judah to prepare for the march. Moses seeing all getting ready for departure, tries to persuade Hobab to accompany them, ostensibly with the sole object of doing him good, and that he may share in Israel's blessings; but having really also another motive, namely, desiring to have the experience and skill of Hobab to assist him in their wilderness journey. "Thou mayest be unto us instead of eyes." This God cannot permit. He is jealous of his people's affections and dependence on Himself. Hobab's knowledge of the wilderness may do where the people of God are not concerned; but it is the presence and guidance of God alone that is to be the security and blessing of His own people. Accordingly, the Ark, jealous, as it were, of this place of watchful and patient care, moves out from its usual position in the centre, and takes the lead of Israel. It is like the skillful general assuming the command, when he sees his forces about to be committed to the care of one whose judgment he cannot trust. This is the first occasion on which the golden staves were used; and here we find this holy vessel passing forward at the head of the people into the trackless desert, to find out a temporary resting-place for them. It was the shepherd of Israel going before the flock, and carefully seeking not only the right path for them, but also a place where He might cause the sheep of His pasture awhile to rest. And for three days is the search continued, till the suited place for repose is found.

This, indeed, tells us of the watchful, considerate thoughtfulness of one who knew the need and weakness of the little ones in the camp. " He shall feed his flock like a shepherd, He shall gather the lambs with his arm, and carry them in his bosom, and shall gently lead those that are with young." (Isa. xf. n.) And His sheep know His voice. They know one who can even now lead them beside the peaceful waters and cause them to lie down in green pastures. One who has all the patient sympathy that is needed to bear with weakness and infirmity, and who uses the strength and wisdom of God thus in the way of gentleness and grace. He is able in the desert even to find out a place for a little timely refreshment and repose, which may give vigour for the future march. The valley of Baca He can make to be a well; "the rain filleth the pools."

Moses seems not to have understood this. Fully conscious of the mighty power of that Ark, he does indeed exclaim when it sets forward, " Rise up, Lord, and let thine enemies be scattered, and let them that hate thee flee before thee." But he little appears to have known the patient, forbearing grace, the gentle skillfulness of Him who dwelt between the Cherubim; and, therefore, he had sought human experience, and human foresight, for the guidance of Israel. And so, will it ever be ignorance of, or want of confidence in, the minute tender care and wisdom of God will end in the arm of flesh being leant on, or the wisdom of man trusted. May we learn increasingly to depend on Him who unites Almighty power and glorious strength with unfailing wisdom, mercy, and grace.

But the Ark having thus taken at unusual place, the cloud gets, as it were, displaced as to its ordinary position in the journey. How rich, however, are the resources of grace, and how skillful! We find the cloud, instead of going before the camp, taking a new place in this beautiful little history; and it is said, " The cloud of the Lord was upon them by day when they went out of the camp." The cloud of the Lord yields the place of guidance to the Ark and retires to be a shelter and covering over them by day to screen them from the fierce smiting sun, and to afford them a refreshing shadow in that dry and weary land. (Psalm cv. 39.) And thus, commenced Israel's journeyings from Sinai; and might not these discoveries of God's rich provisions of mercy and watchful care have made them even value the wilderness itself, because it drew forth such varied and blessed displays of the Lord? And may not the believer also find that his hand can bring out of the eater sweetness ; and that the very trials and sorrows of the way shall only be occasions for fresh exhibitions of his gentleness and love, and of the rich and varied resources of his grace, who is with him all the journey through, to be his shepherd, his guide, his counsellor, his defense, his protector? True, the journey will be one of tribula- tion ; Israel found that they got out of one wilderness only to get into another (Num. x. 12): there may be differences in the prospect around, but it is a wilderness still, and the main features of a wilderness will always present gloom, and barrenness, and desolation ; yet may not the soul be so occupied with God, so delighted in marking His wondrous love, so habituated to watch His hand and His ways, that the very difficulties and dangers of the path become to it but signals for His appearance, and it finds its own joy and triumph in His exercise of wisdom, mercy, and power. An apostle could even boast of his infirmities, that the power of Christ might rest upon him. The same Ark that had thus, at the commencement of the journey, proved itself the careful guardian and patient guide of Israel in their weakness, stood forth yet once again at the close, to

lead Israel in triumph into the land of their rest Once again, at the distance of nearly forty years, it put itself at the head of Israel's hosts ; and the deep waters of the swollen Jordan fled from before it, and the lofty walls of Jericho tottered and fell down at its presence. The same one who knew how " to carry the lambs in his bosom, and gently lead those that were with young," could put forth, when it was needed, the irresistible might of the Cherubim of glory. Israel's last journeying was now over, and behold them at length, after forty years' wanderings, encamped close to the Jordan, and resting there for a while before they enter the land. The river had burst its bounds and rolled on its sullen and deep waters before them, an effectual barrier, apparently, to their entering the land of their rest. But the Ark of the Covenant of their God was with them, and could again point out the trackless path to them, even through the deep waters, and could not only mark out the way, but make the difficult and dangerous path easy and safe for their footsteps: they were to observe its steps, "that they might know the way by which they must go, for they had not passed that way heretofore." (Josh. iii. 4.) Silently the Ark moved on, and Israel halted at a fitting distance to mark its progress. The deep and rolling stream seemed to defy its advance, but no sooner did the feet of the priests that bare the Ark but touch the brim of the water, than the affrighted river rose up, and fled in dismay; back and back were the descending waters driven upon themselves, till a huge piled-up heap afar off, out of sight, betokened the Almighty power of that arm which had hurled back the impetuous stream, and had, as it were, congealed the depths in the midst of the waters. "What ailed thee, thou Jordan, that thou wast driven back?" (Psalm cxiv. 3, 5.)
" And the priests that bare the Ark of the Covenant of the Lord stood firm on dry ground in the midst of Jordan, and all the Israelites passed over on dry ground, until all the people were passed clean over Jordan." (J*9sh. iii. 17.) And shall we not ourselves realise shortly such a scene as this? Or rather a scene, compared with which this is but a faint shadow. Will not that hand which now patiently waits upon our necessities, and oftentimes smooths the rugged path, be stretched out ere long in terrible majesty, to rescue the Church from all the power of sin, Satan, and death, and to guide them by His strength into His holy habitation?

Yes, the day of resurrection, the day of the Lord s return, when He, the captain of salvation, will put Himself at the head of His risen saints, to lead them into the mansions of their eternal glory, will manifest the uncontrollable might of Him who now deals with them in patient, unwearied grace.

The command of the Lord respecting the staves was, that they were not to be taken from the Ark. (Exod. xxv. 15.) They were to remain in the rings, as a proof that there was an adaptation of the Ark to the whole period of wandering and conflict, through which Israel had to pass previous to their final rest in the land ; and the Ark was thus ever at hand, and prepared to be their guide or their defense in every circumstance of difficulty. But at length we read of a time having arrived when, with the Lord's sanction, these staves were finally drawn out. When the wilderness journey being over, and every enemy subdued, the Ark could enter into its rest, and the staves could therefore safely be withdrawn, seeing there would be similar seasons of wandering and conflict no more. The occasion of bringing up the Ark into the final place prepared for it is beautifully described in 1 Kings viii. and 2 Chron. v. The reign of him, who is eminently the type of the Prince of Peace, had commenced ; the enemies of the Lord had been subdued, and just retribution had fallen upon the heads of the apostates and unfaithful amongst Israel, and after seven years of noiseless labour the house of the Lord had been erected at Jerusalem, and all was now prepared for the reception of the Ark into the mo t holy place.

The season chosen for this joyful event was the feast of the seventh month, the Feast of Tabernacles, when Israel had to appear before the Lord at Jerusalem, to rejoice before Him in the full fruition of present blessings, contrasted with the remembrance of their former season of toil and conflict, now ended forever. It was the closing feast of the year, when all the rich fruits of the land had been gathered in, when the winepress and corn floor were full, and the Lord had prospered them in the basket and the store : in the midst of all this festivity and abundance they were however again to take a kind of wilderness position, and to dwell seven days in booths, that they might call to mind the time when, as poor wanderers out of Egypt, they had been cast upon the watchful mercy of the Lord ; who had succoured them and led them, with all his shepherd care, and had guided them by His strength into their land of rest and blessing. Thus their very first encampment ("Succoth" — booths), when the remembrance of the blood of the paschal lamb was fresh in their thoughts, and when, for the first time, released from the thraldom and bondage of Egypt, they were cast in their helplessness on the merciful care of God, was to be recorded in their last annual feast of joy in the land of promise. This was the season chosen for bringing up the Ark into the Temple ; and there are circumstances recorded throughout that scene that clearly point onward to a season of joy and blessing yet future, both to the Church of God in resurrection, and to Israel here- after on the earth. For there is a time shortly to come when the whole Church of God will, like Israel of old, have finished its wilderness journey; when its last conflict will be over, its toilsome march ended; and when, raised by Almighty power, it will stand, as seen in Rev. vii., around the throne of God and the Lamb, celebrating in the glory, as it were, its Feast of Tabernacles. The robe washed white in the blood of the Lamb, betokening the full cleansing of the Sanctuary, enabling that countless multitude to minister in the heavenly courts as priests, all consecrated, all sanctified, all able to enter into the most holy places ; none waiting by course, but all able to serve. (2 Chron. v. 11.) The branches of palm in their hands, as records of a wilderness passed through, and trophies thence gleaned of a complete and eternal triumph, seem to indicate that one spring of joy in that blessed rest will be the remembrance of the past, contrasted with the present full and bright scenes of glory. The elder, who looked with the apostle on that scene, marks in his answer to the latter this contrast. He refers to their past wanderings in the desert, and contrasts with that season of toil and privation their present rest in the temple of God. "They shall hunger no more, neither thirst anymore; neither shall the sun light on them, nor any heat ;" — true experiences these of the wilder- ness they had passed through ; — "for the Lamb which is in the midst of the throne shall feed them, and shall lead them unto living fountains of waters, and God shall wipe away all tears from their eyes." Then, indeed, will the staves be needed no more in the Ark ; for, as regards the Church, its every conflict will be ended, and its full and eternal rest will have been gained : the present ministration of Christ, known now to us as our strength in weakness, our guide in difficulties, our help in need, our power of victory over temptation, will be required then no more. His heart will then be able fully to rest in looking on us ; " He will see of the travail of his soul, and will be satisfied;" yea, He will be satisfied with us, and "will present us before the presence of his glory with exceeding joy." And surely it will be one chief part of our joy in that day to look upon Him, and feel that we are part of His glory and of His joy; and to usher Him, as it were, into His own rest, conscious that our wants, our follies, our weaknesses, will disturb it no more; but that He can fully rest and rejoice over us, as presented to God in His own perfectness, and fitted to minister as kings and priests to His God and Father.

But the staves, though drawn out, were not removed (1 Kings viii. 8); they were still kept in the most holy place, though no longer needed. And does not this teach us that the patient and gracious ministry of Christ, as now accompanying His Church in all its journeys and battles with the enemy, will no longer be needed when it has entered the glory, yet that the remembrance of it will still be carefully preserved there? Surely, we shall even there learn deep lessons of His love, when we look back and retrace the path trodden here by us, with Jesus by our side ; the difficulties surmounted through His aid, the steps restored through His going down into our need to lift us up, the grace of one who has been with us in all our wanderings, "been afflicted in all our afflictions:" it may be many a deliverance, many a healing, many an act of sovereign mercy and love, unknown or unheeded by us now, will in that day be discovered, and cause the song of joy and thanks-giving to arise with increased power. And though all that might cause a pang or a regret will be gone forever, yet all that will enhance our value of the grace of Jesus will be gladly brought to mind ; and deeply will it instruct us in His love to retrace the way in which He has borne with our waywardness, and forgetfulness, and evil, and carried us, as on eagles' wings, through every danger and failure, triumphantly into His rest In this scene other types of the glory of the latter day may be also observed : we have Israel represented as sacrificing sheep and oxen before the Ark, which could not be told nor numbered for multitude, whilst the priests usher the Ark into its final place of rest. This seems to be a beautiful millennial scene. Israel on earth fully appreciating the value of the sacrifice, reckoning it, indeed, beyond all that can be numbered ; the heavenly priesthood, the glorious company of the risen saints, ushering the Ark of God's strength into the holy of holies, accompanying and welcoming the Lord Jesus into the heaven of heavens, and the song of joy and thanksgiving bursting forth from the heavenly and earthly family alike, with one voice, with one sound, praising the Lord in one blessedly simple, and yet deep and eternal, strain of truth, " For He is good, for his mercy endureth forever." Then the glory of the Lord manifesting itself to Israel, the full blessing of His presence among them, and the priests themselves suspending their ministry, because the very end and object of their ministry was accomplished, namely, the manifested glory of Jehovah in the midst of His people ; — are not these intimations of scenes of glory and blessing yet before us, which we may do well to contemplate in hope? — scenes that will suddenly burst upon us at the coming of the Lord, the expectation of which would greatly tend to separate our hearts from all that passes around us on earth now, and to strengthen us to endure with patience the little that yet remains of the wilderness path to be trodden by the redeemed of the Lord.

It is a question often asked, Why there was nothing in the Ark when it was deposited in the Temple but the two tables of stone, seeing that during the wilder- ness journey Moses had put also into the Ark the golden pot that had manna, and Aaron's rod that budded? (Heb. ix. 4.) It seems as if the direct declaration, twice repeated (1 Kings viii. 9; 2 Chron. v. 10), that there was nothing in the Ark save the tables of the covenant, has some truth contained in it to which the Spirit would guide our thoughts, and it may be the object is to lead us to mark the scene thus depicted, as one eminently typical of the world to come.

The manna laid up in the golden pot is called, in Rev. ii. 17, "the hidden manna," and a promise is there given that he that overcometh shall eat thereof. Christ is already known to and fed upon by believers as the true bread from heaven. His flesh and blood is the daily sustainment of the life of the saint, as trie first eating of that flesh and blood was the communication of life. As thus known, the gift of God to us for life and sustainment, He is the manna that came down from heaven; but there is also the "hidden manna;" and this seems to allude to Christ, yet to be known as the food of the saint in glory. We now know Him only in part, then we shall know even as we are known, we now see through a glass darkly, but then face to face. " We shall see him as he is." During this our wilderness time the manna daily is provided for us, and Christ is known to us as food adapted to our wilderness state ; but there is manna now stored up and hidden in the presence of God for us, which shall be dispensed to us when we enter the glory ; and the scene in Kings and Chronicles, which we have been considering, seems to point on to that time, when the manna therefore will be no longer hidden in the Ark, but when there will be the full, unhindered knowledge of Christ, known face to face to His risen saints.

Aaron's rod, also, was no longer in the Ark at the time of which we speak. The reason for which may be as follows: — Israel had previously to their entering the land questioned God's appointed priesthood, and had murmured at the judgment of God which had fallen on those who had, uncalled for, and unappointed by Him, thrust themselves into the holy service. The Lord in His grace took this method of stilling their murmurings. He commanded twelve rods to be laid up before Him, with every man's name upon his rod, according to the house of their fathers. "And it shall come to pass that the man's rod whom I shall choose shall blossom; and I will make to cease from me the murmurings of the children of Israel, whereby they murmur against you." (Num. xvii. 1-11.)

The rod of Aaron, thus laid up before the Lord, was found on the morrow to have budded, and brought forth buds, and bloomed blossoms, and yielded almonds. This was God's mode of vindicating his priest. And this has been his way of vindicating Him, who now stands in heaven as our great High Priest The dry twig, cut off from all nourishment, withered in death, has found these circumstances of darkness and ruin to be the very soil, as it* were, from whence it should spring forth as the fruitful bough. Jesus disowned by Israel and cut off out of the land of the living, has sprung up out of the grave — the branch, in the full vigour and maturity of life, and with an eternal prospect of fruitfulness yet to come. Buds, blossoms, and ripe fruit, all at once found upon the almond rod, betokened a full maturity of strength and beauty, as well as a further development of life and power, which render it an apt emblem of Him, who rose from the dead in all the freshness, and yet in all the perfectness, and ripeness of new creation. No eye but that of God rested on the rod laid up before Him ; it remained all night shut up, and life was thus under His eye produced out of death, and the dry and withered rod was in the morning seen to be full of life, fruitfulness, and beauty. But this rod was subsequently hidden in the Ark, kept there as a token against the rebels, but still as a sure presage that all their murmuring should eventually be quite taken away. And so now this risen one, fruitful in resurrection, is hidden from Israel's eye, the great token indeed against and proof of Israel's rebellion ; but still the steady witness before God that the day will come, when, through Him, God will cause all their murmuring and unbelief to cease forever. In the scene, therefore, in Kings and Chronicles, which looks on to that time, no mention is made of Aaron's rod, or rather it is purposely excluded, because, when that scene is fulfilled, the rebellious nation will have been brought into its final blessing, and Christ and the heavenly priesthood will have been fully owned. The " hidden manna," the food of the risen saints, will be hidden no more ; and He that is typified by "the rod that budded," will manifestly stand forth in all the power, glory, and beauty of the heavenly priesthood.

THE THRONE OF GRACE.

"And there I will meet with thee, and I will commune with thee from above the Mercy Seat, from between the two cherubims which are upon the Ark of the testimony, of all things which I will give thee in commandment unto the children of Israel" (Exod. xxv. 22.) "And when Moses was gone into the Tabernacle of the congre- gation to speak with him, then he heard the voice of one speaking unto him from off the ftjercy Seat that was upon the Ark of testimony, from between the two cherubims. (Num. vii. 89.)

Thus Moses was to approach the Lord at the Mercy Seat, and to receive from thence directions and commandments from Him ; and subsequently Aaron, after the sin of Nadab and Abihu, was forbidden from coming in thither, except once a year, when he was to draw nigh with the blood of atonements in his hand. So that Moses and Aaron alone had access to the Mercy Seat; the one to get commandments, the other to atone for sin. How contrasted with this is the use of the true Mercy Seat to the believer! He knows it as the " Throne of Grace," not a throne of judgment, or from whence commandments are given, but from whence pity and grace are dispensed. A throne, where indeed God is known, in His glorious holiness, but yet where all speaks of atonement already made; of salvation already accomplished; of full, unmixed favour flowing unhindered from God. Aaron must have approached with dread; he had to present blood for himself, as well as for the sins of the people. In the very act of thus going in, he had to call sin to remembrance ; and what if in some part of the prescribed ritual he had failed? judgment and wrath might break out against him, as before it had burst forth against his own sons Nadab and Abihu. But the believer's access is with boldness — and not only once a year, but at all times, "in every time of need:" every hour, every moment, it is his blessed privilege to enter there and hold intercourse with God; and there pity as well as grace awaits him ; there sympathy, as well as needful help, is granted. He fears not the want of fitness in himself, for he knows that in Christ alone is his fitness for God's most holy presence ; he fears not his sins as disqualifying him ; for that blessed place Where God is known as " light in whom is no darkness at all," is the place where the blood of atonement has already been sprinkled, and by a blood-sprinkled path also can he enter: indeed, it is the very consciousness of his need that bids him with confidence draw near.

Satan would fain keep our souls away from this place of blessing, would fain interrupt our communion and intercourse with God. The tempter often suggests arguments for our staying away from this throne of grace. " You have failed, you have sinned, you have neglected or abused God's mercy, and therefore you are not fit to draw near ; you must wait till you are in a better state, till you have proved the reality of your love for God, for now you have not the same title to approach God as once you had:" these and such like suggestions are often whispered in our hearts by the enemy of souls. But what is all this reasoning really but mistrust of the grace of God, and ignorance or doubt as to His character, and of the value of Jesus? If a believer has sinned, it is in God's presence, and not afar off, that he must judge the sin. It is in the light of God's unchanging love alone that he will be able to estimate at all the depth of his own ingratitude and evil ; it is when the value of the blood is fully known that the believer can alone rightly appreciate the darkness and malignity of that sin which needed such blood. And surely there is no time of greater need, no occasion when the throne of grace is more really required, than when the believer has, for a while, been wandering from the right path. It is too often the habit of the children of God to wait till time has blunted the conscience as to any sin into which they may have fallen, before they venture again into the presence of God; and when the soul has got a measure of calmness restored by reason of the deadening effect of time, they fancy they are better able thereby to approach God. Whereas the truth is, that to stay away from the presence of God is to continue unhumbled on account of sin : real lowliness and contrition of spirit will alone be found in the consciousness of the glory and holiness, as well as grace, of His presence.

Faith has to be exercised as much (it may be more) in the soul of a saint that has failed, in restoring or sustaining his confidence in God, as in sustaining him above failure. The Lord had prayed for

Simon that his faith might not fail and bid him watch and pray lest he should enter into temptation. This Peter failed to do, and in the natural, heedless ardour of his character, and ignorant of his own weakness, he thrust himself into the very place of temptation, when, as might have been expected, he sinned again and again with fearful deliberateness ; but directly he met the eye of Jesus, $he prayer of the Lord for him was proved to be effectual ; his faith failed not ; he left the scene of temptation at once, bitterly indeed sorrowing over his sin, but never for a moment mistrusting the grace of Him against whom he had so grievously sinned. We find him, therefore, t^e first to run towards the sepulchre, the first to enter in and search for Him whom he bad wronged ; and subsequently at the lake of Gennesaret, (that very lake where he had first known himself a sinner in the presence of the Lord,) directly he gets an intimation from John that it was Jesus who stood on the shore, he is the first to cast himself into the sea, regardless of his danger, and eager to be foremost to welcome Him. Here was faith that failed not — faith that could reckon largely on grace, that at once enabled Peter to seek and welcome the Lord, that taught him that access to the throne of pity and of grace was ever open. The following is a brief outline of the history of the Ark as recorded in Scripture: — Sinai. Directions given by the Lord to Moses for its being made Where to be placed — in the Most Holy. Moses directs the children of Israel to make the Ark, &c. Bezaleel makes it Brought to Moses by the children of Israel The Tables of Testimony put into it by Moses. Deut. x. 1-5. Placed in the Tabernacle by Moses. To be the meeting-place between the Lord and Moses. Num vii. 89. .... To be anointed with the holy oil Anointed when the Priests are consecrated not to be approached by Aaron at all times. The blood to be' sprinkled on the Mercy Seat, and before the Mercy Seat, once a year — on the great day of atonement Under the charge of the Kohathites the coverings of the Ark previous to the march The ordinary place of the Ark in the march The Wilderness. The Ark departs from its ordinary place and leads the way. The first journey from Sinai ...The Ark abides in the camp during the discomfiture of the Israelites at Hormah .....Aaron's rod laid up before it From Heb. ix. 4, we learn that this rod, as well as the pot of manna, were placed inside the Ark It seems to have gone up to battle with Israel under Phinehas, as "holy instruments," as well as the silver trumpets, are mentioned ...... Moses directs the Levites to place the Book of the Law inside the Ark . Exod. xxv. 10-22. Exod. xxvi. 34 ; xl. 3.Exod. xxxv. 12. Exod. xxxvii. 1-9. Exod. xxxix. 35. Exod. xl. 20. Exod. xl. 21. Exod. xxv. 22. Exod. xxx. 26 ; xl. 9. Lev. viii. 10. Lev. xvi. 2, &c Num. iii. 31. Num. iv. 5, 6. Num. x. 21. Num. x. 33-36. Num. xiv. 44. Num. xvii. 10. Num. xxxi. 6. Deut. xxxi. 9-26. The Land. The Ark divides the waters of Jordan . . . Josh. iii. and iv. The walls of Jericho fall down before the Ark . . Josh, vi. Israel defeated at Ai. Joshua falls on the earth before the Ark. God directs him as to Achan .... Josh. vii. The Ark stands between Ebal and Gerizim, whilst the blessings and curses are pronounced. Deut. xxvii. 11-26. . Josh. viii. 30-35.

GILGAL.

Joshua holds a standing camp at Gilgal, from whence he makes various excursions and conquests of the land. Josh. xiv. 6. — Here also he divides some portions of the land amongst Israel. Hence it is probable that the Tabernacle and Ark were here for a time ...... Josh. ix. 6; x. 7-43. Shiloh. The Tabernacle at length removed to Shiloh, and formally set up there. Josh, xviii. and xix. — The remainder of the land divided, xxi. — Levitical cities appointed, xxii. 9.— The two and a half tribes sent back. xxii. 12. — Israel assembles here respecting the altar of the Reubenites. Hence it is probable that the Ark was in the Tabernacle all the time it was at Shiloh . . Josh, xviii. Shechem.

Subsequently we find Joshua gathering all Israel to Shechem, and that " the sanctuary of the Lord " was there. But the Ark may have remained at Shiloh, as the Tabernacle was replaced there again before the time of Jud. xx. . . . . . . Josh. xxiv. I-26. Shiloh. The Tabernacle and Ark again stationary here, as is evident from the 4 'house of God," twice mentioned, Jud. xx. 18, 26; and the Ark also in connection with it, ver. 27. That this was at Shiloh seems plain, from xxi. 2, 12, 19. And I Sam. i. opens with worship and sacrifice carried on at Shiloh. I Sam. iii. 3. — The Ark directly mentioned as at Shiloh. Aphek and Ebenezer. The Ark fetched by Israel to the battle and is captured by the Philistines. See also Psalm lxxviii. 60, 61. . . . 1 Sam. iv. Ash do d. The Ark removed by the Philistines from Ebenezer to Ashdod. 1 Sam. v. 1-8. — In the house of Dagon at Ashdod. Dagon falls before it. . . . .1 Sam. v. 1. Ekron. The Ark sent to Ekron. The Philistines plague. 1 Sam. v. 8-12; vi. 1-2. Beth-shemesh. The Ark sent dp in a new cart, takes the way to Beth-shemesh. The men of Beth-shemesh slain, because they looked into the Ark I Sam. vi. 9 20. KlRJATH-JEARIM. The Ark taken to Kirjath-jearim, and remains there twenty years I Sam. vi. 21 ; vii. 1, 2 i6

GlBEAH.

Saul consults the Ark in Gibeah at the time of Jonathan's miraculous success ; but it must have been only removed from Kirjath-jearim for a time, as we find it again there, 2 Sam. vi. ... I Sam. xiv. 1 6- 1 8. Kirjath-jearim, called also Baale of Judah and Gibeah. The Ark fetched up thence by David out of the house of Abinadab, where it had been twenty years. In 2 Sam. vi. the house of Abinadab is said to be in Gibeah, but this only means "the hill;" see I Sam. vii. I. 2 Sam. vi. The House of Obed-edom. Uzzah smitten, and the Ark is carried aside into the house of Obed-edom, the Gittite. 2 Sam. vi. II ; I Chron. xiii. 14. — It remains there three months. The City of David, or Jerusalem, or Zion.

David prepares a place for the Ark, and a tent for it, in the city of David. 2 Sam. vi. 12-23; I Chron. xv. 1-29 ; xvi. 1-3. — He carries it up on the shoulders of the Levites to the city of David, and deposits it in the Tabernacle he had made for it. I Chron. xvi. 4-38. — Levites appointed to minister before the Ark . . . . . .1 Chron. xv. I.

(The Tabernacle and altar of burnt-offering were at this time at Gibeon, and remained there till Solomon removed it and its vessels to the Temple. I Chron. xvi. 39; xxi. 29. 1 Kings iii. 4- 1 5. 2 Chron. i. 3-13. 1 Kings viii. 4.) David desires to build a house for the Ark but is not permitted. I Chron. xvii. I. . . . . 2 Sam. vii. 2. David sins in the matter of Bathsheba. Uriah refuses to take his rest in his own house, because the Ark and Israel are abiding in tents 2 Sam. xi. II.

David obliged to flee from Jerusalem, because of Absalom's rebellion, and sends back Zadok and the Levites with the Ark to Jerusalem, after they had accom- panied him a little way .... 2 Sam. xv. 24, 25, &c. Solomon builds the Temple on Mount Moriah. . 2 Chron. iii. 1. 1 Kings vi. 1, &c. The oracle for the Ark, with two colossal cherubim . . 1 Kings vi. 19, 23-28.

Mount Moriah.

The Ark is borne from the city of David, or Mount Zion, to its resting-place in the Temple, on Mount Moriah ; and the staves are drawn out. 2 Chron. v. I Kings viii. We hear no more of the Ark till the time of Josiah, when it seems as if it had been previously moved from the Temple but was replaced there by his command. (2 Chron. xxxv. 3.)

" When that which is perfect is come, then that which is in part shall be done away.'* " And it shall come to pass when ye be multiplied and increased in the land in those days, saith the Lord, they shall say no more, The Ark of the covenant of the Lord; neither shall it come to mind, neither shall they remember it, neither shall they visit it, neither shall that be done any more. At that time they shall call Jerusalem the throne of the Lord ; and all the nations shall be gathered unto it, to the name of the Lord, to Jerusalem : neither shall they walk any more after the imagination of their evil heart." (Jer. iii. 16, 17.)

NOTES TO THE ARK AND MERCY SEAT.

The following are the names

Ark of the Lord. Josh. iv. 11, etc.
Ark of the God of Israel. I Sam. v. 7, etc.

Ark of God. 1 Sam. iii. 3.
Ark of thy strength. Psalm cxxxii. 8.
The holy Ark. 2 Chron. xxxv. 3.

1 The Hebrew word }P1*, translated " Ark," means a "chest.' or designations attached to the Ark : — Ark of the Testimony. Exod. xxv. 22, etc. Ark of the Covenant of the Lord. Num. x. 33, etc. Ark of the Covenant of God. Judges xx. 27. Ark of the Covenant. Josh. iii. 6. Ark of the Lord, the lord of all the earth. Josh. iii. 13.

2 Some have supposed that the Book of the Law mentioned in Deut. xxxi. 26, as put in the side of the Ark, was "the Testimony;" but this is clearly not the case, for the Testimony is expressly stated as above (Exod. xl. 20) to have been put into the Ark at its first formation. "The Testimony " is sometimes used for the whole vessel, Ark and Mercy Seat, inclosing the Tables of the Covenant, as Exodus xxvii. 21; xxx. 36. The word Testimony occurs attached to—
The Ark . . Exod. xxv. 22 . . " The Ark of the Testimony." The Tables . Exod. xxxii. 15 . "The two Tables of the Testimony." The Vail . . Lev. xxiv. 3 . . . "The Vail of the Testimony." The Tent . Num. ix. 15 . . " The Tent of the Testimony." 3 In Deut. x. 1-5, we have the history of Moses descending from the mount the second time, and immediately putting the tables of stone into the Ark, as if fearing to expose them for a moment in the midst of Israel. This must evidently be read as a kind of commentary on the history as given in Exodus ; for, in point of fact, as we there read, the Ark was not made till after Moses had descended the second time from the mount, and could not, therefore, have been at hand to receive the tables at once. But in reading other parts of the history of the Tabernacle, and the institution of the priesthood connected with it, we shall find that the only way to understand many of the statements is on the ground that different narratives of the same events are written with different aspects, to instruct in typical truth rather than to give a connected or consecutive history of the events as they occurred. And is not this especially to be borne in mind, also, in reading and comparing the different narratives of the gospels?

* The explanation of these symbolic faces of the Cherubim is chiefly taken from a beautiful paper on the subject, entitled "The Vision of the Glory of God," printed in the 1st volume of the " Christian Witness." It will be seen that the Staves are in the drawings placed sideways, and not lengthways in the Ark. This seems to be their right position, because it is not probable that the Ark would be turned about, when it was taken up to be carried in the journeys but would be borne straightforward. Also, from I Kings viii. 8, it would appear that, when drawn out of the rings, the Staves reached forwards towards the holy place ; and the high priest, when taking in the incense and blood on the great day of atonement, would (if this were the position of the Staves) go in between them up to the Mercy Scat, instead of going up as it were against one of them.

THE SHEWBREAD TABLE.

EX XXV 23 30- f-^. W O/CHCS. UTH LO*OOH
objects would allow- »n or lion, dall here there.; the table strength md a over- unto a made round order four. four Over *s for the with ark-

THE TABLE

THE calling of the Church is to have fellowship with God — to have subjects of interest, affection, and joy, in common with Him — and that in every sphere of divine glory. Adam, unfallen in the garden, had around him objects in which he could take delight with God. All creation had been formed and pronounced " very good," and Adam could have fellowship with God in the works of His hands. But this was only a very limited sphere of blessing. To know God as the Creator of all that was around, to see and understand the fitness and beauty of all that God had made, was after all but a distant knowledge of God, and but a very limited acquaintance with His ways. But even this man lost when he fell; instead of having intercourse with God, and knowing Him as once he might, he turns from Him, and hides himself in the trees of the garden from His presence. He thus acknowledges that there is no common ground on which he might stand and meet God, and that all happy intercourse, and all subjects of happy fellowship with God, have been forfeited ; and that his only hope of rest and quiet is to get away from His presence. And such is man by nature — still distant from God, and only at ease as long as he can keep at a distance, and having no objects or desires in common with God — " God is not in all his thoughts." u But now, in Christ Jesus, ye who sometimes were far off are made nigh by the blood of Christ;" and not only have we access and nearness to God, but "truly our fellowship is with the Father, and with His Son Jesus Christ." The Church of God has been redeemed out of the world and taken up into the heavenlies, there to know by faith unhindered access to God, and there to find communion with the Father and the Son. The Ark with its golden cover, the Mercy Seat, was, as we have seen, typical of the Throne of Grace established in the heavens, where we meet the God of glory, and from whence He dispenses His blessings to His people. But this did not necessarily constitute a place of communion with God. A king might erect an audience chamber and throne, where he might receive the homage of his subjects, and from whence he might dispense gifts, and rewards, and honours; but it would not follow that there was any fellowship between himself and his people. Fellow- ship implies that there are common interests, and common objects of affection or pursuit. A table is especially a place of friendly intercourse and communion. There blessings are enjoyed and partaken of in common between the head and all the members of the family ; there the same food is spread alike before all ; and there the same sources of refreshment and joy are alike presented to all associated together.

We have then in this second vessel of the Tabernacle a place of fellowship; the description of it is as follows: — Exod. xxv. 23-28. — Thou shalt also make a table of shittim wood: two cubits shall be the length thereof, and a cubit the breadth thereof, and a cubit and a half the height thereof. And thou shalt overlay it with pure gold and make thereto a crown of gold round about. And thou shalt make unto it a border of a hand -breadth round about, and thou shalt make a golden crown to the border thereof round about. And thou shalt make for it four rings of gold and put the rings in the four corners that are on the four feet thereof. Over against the border shall the rings be for places of the staves to bear the table. And thou shalt make the staves of shittim wood, and overlay them with gold, that the table may be borne with them. |

The Table of Shewbread was thus made of the same materials as the Ark- wood overlaid with gold. Here again we have a type of the Lord Jesus as God 1 Exod. xxxvii. 10-15. — And he made the table of shittim wood : two cubits zvas the length thereof, and a cubit the breadth thereof, and a cubit and a half the height thereof : and he over- laid it with pure gold, and made thereunto a crown of gold round about. Also, he made thereunto a border of an handbreadth round about, and made a crown of gold for the border thereof round about. And he cast for it four rings of gold and put the rings upon the four corners that were in the four feet thereof. Over against the border were the rings, the places for the staves to bear the table. And he made the staves of shittim wood, and overlaid them with gold, to bear the table. the Lord Jesus as God and man in one person, sustaining another office of priestly ministration. It was needful, in order that He might be the priest, that He should be man; but his priesthood is after no human order. Melchisedec, of which order Christ has been constituted priest, was one, in the Scripture, suddenly presented before us, as without father or mother, without pedigree, without any specification of age, or birth, or death ; and stands, therefore, as a type of the Son of God Himself. And it is after this eternal and divine order of priesthood that Christ has arisen ; attach- ing divine and eternal power, value, and glory to all He is and does as priest; whilst at the same time He can, as man, truly stand as the representative of the redeemed, and feels real and full sympathy for them. The gold is of a different substance, a different material from the wood; but it adds preciousness, firmness, and eternal stability and glory to the wood.

THE DIMENSIONS OF THE TABLE.

The golden Table thus formed is specified as to its dimensions to have been two cubits in length, one cubit in breadth, and a cubit and a half in height The measures of the holy vessels, and of the Tabernacle and its courts, are ail doubtless intended to be significant, and are interesting subjects of inquiry as to their typical import. Without being at present able to affix any definite meaning to these numbers, it may however be suggested, whether the dimensions of the Ark do not afford a kind of standard with which we may compare the other measurements ; and whether the relative size of the other vessels has not reference to the size of the Ark, or some connection with, or dependence on, its magnitude. May there not, in the size thus specified of the Shewbread Table, be an intention of drawing our thoughts to the fact of its being of the same height with the Ark, though less in length and breadth ? and may not this imply that there is a presentation to God in Christ of human perfectness, elevated as high as His own throne, and sustained under the full blaze of His glory? and whilst the length and breadth of the Ark and Mercy Seat are larger, may it not be intended to convey to us the thought of the wider presentation of God's grace as seen in Christ, the one Mediator between God and men — the extensive aspect of His mercy and love ?

THE BREAD ON THE TABLE.

We find in Lev. xxiv. 5, 6, directions given respecting the bread to be placed on the table. " And thou shalt take fine flour, and bake twelve cakes thereof: two SHEWBREAD. tenth deals shall be in one cake. And thou shalt set them in two rows, six on a row, upon the pure table before the Lord." " Fine flour" was the material of which these cakes were to be made. This is also commanded in Lev. ii. as the great constituent part of the meat-offering; and we have the direct authority of the word itself for saying that the meat-offering was a type of Christ; for it is written in Psalm xl. 6-8, " Sacrifice and offering thou didst not desire; mine ears hast thou opened: burnt-offering and sin-offering hast thou not required. Then said I, Lo, I come in the volume of the book it is written of me, I delight to do thy will, O my God: yea, thy law is within my heart." Here all the four principal offerings of the book of Leviticus are enumerated : the peace-sacrifice, the meat-offering, the burnt-offering, and the sin-offering ; and all are declared to be in themselves valueless to God, and superseded by one whose ears had been "digged" by God to be His servant, and who was coming to do His will, and of whom in the volume of the book it had been all written. The roll of the book of Leviticus, or of the law, had indeed all been written of Christ ; and in fulfilling the will of God He fulfilled every jot and tittle of these varied offerings, all which were but shadows pointing on to Him who is the substance. (Heb. x.; Col. ii. 17.) In the 10th of Hebrews, where this psalm is quoted, we have a remarkable change of the sentence, "mine ears hast thou opened" into "a body hast thou prepared me:" a blessed commentary on, and an illustration of, the passage by the Spirit of

God Himself, teaching us that the opening the ears of the Lord to be the servant of Jehovah, or, as one has elsewhere suggested, the digging or nailing the ear to the door in token of servitude, was equivalent to the preparing Christ a body, and sending Him down here on earth as the "word made flesh," to walk through the path of human life in true humble obedience, ending at last in obedience unto death, even the death of the cross. The meat-offering, then, and shewbread were alike written of Christ, and were fulfilled as to their typical import by His coming in the flesh to do the will of God ; the body being prepared for Him by God, and the listening ear thus formed, that He might, as the servant, obey God perfectly on earth. The fine flour of which both were composed is indeed a beautiful and expressive type of that pure and perfect man who thus came to do the Father's will. It represents Him as in the flesh, because the fine flour is a product of the earth, grown, and nurtured, and ripened here; and we know the Lord spake of Himself as the corn of wheat, and that with especial reference to His life on earth. But here it is fine Jiour, designating the lowly, unobtrusive, even character of the Lord, not needing to be bruised, but already, at its very outset, having all the characteristics of fine flour ; not needing a course of discipline or chastisement in order to break down harshness or asperities — in Him there were none ; there was no ruggedness, no unevenness ; no starting up of pride or self-exaltation, as if some portion of the whole were not fine and smooth : with Him, from His very birth, all was pure, and even, and lowly— all was tempered and subdued to an even fineness, as to its intrinsic nature ; and a life of sorrow and toil for others' sakes but the more developed and proved the native pre- ciousness and beauty of this heaven-born plant, thus marvellously connected with earth.

We know how to estimate and value the gentleness and grace which is seen in the servants of God around us : this is in them generally the result of long and often painful discipline, and of much exercise of soul before God ; and even when most developed in the saints, how quickly the evil and un-subject nature of the flesh again shows itself, and how it has to be watched against, and incessantly suspected and restrained ! How much, also, of that which wears the appearance of lowliness and humility is the result only of habit, or the effect of an anxious desire to appear in the eyes of others what a Christian ought to be! But blessedly contrasted with all this effort and semblance was His character, who at His very entrance into the world was " that holy thing," who began His life below in self-abasement and humi- lity, tie came here at the cost of all His own glory, laying it aside, and making Himself poor ; proving, by the very fact of His being here, the lowliness of His character, and His simple humble obedience to His God. His birth into this world was the making Himself of no reputation, and He enters on life here below in the likeness of men, and therefore in the form of a servant — the lowly, unobtrusive, obedient servant of God.

But this fine flour was to be baked into twelve cakes before presented on the table. And He that came into the world as the fine flour, had to pass through trials, sorrows, and temptations, during His path below. Satan's temptations, and scorn and rejection from men, deep sorrow on account of the sin and hardness of men's hearts around Him, characterised the path this holy one had to tread on earth ; and yet in blessed obedience and perfectness of heart He could still say, " I delight to do thy will, O my God : yea, thy law is within my heart." These trials and experi- ences of soul, through which He thus passed, added indeed no fresh features of perfectness to His already perfect character ; the fine flour was so intrinsically, but the purity, the lowliness, the grace, and evenness of His character were manifested by means of .the path of sorrow and trial through which He had to pass. His obedience, His perfectness, His dependence on God were thus in every way tested and brought to light ; and at length the cross, with its lonely hours of suffering and sorrow, manifested to the full the wondrous depth of the love and subjection of His heart, " who thus became obedient unto death, even the death of the cross." And in that marvellous closing scene of the life on earth of this spotless one, what ac- cumulated grace and perfectness was then exhibited before God! Brought down in the consciousness of real and yet voluntary degradation to exclaim, " I am a worm and no man — a reproach of men and despised of the people," yet with an unchanged heart of deep and lasting love to Him who had there of necessity forsaken Him (strange though it seemed to be thus forsaken when most obedient), He adds, " But thou art holy, O thou that inhabitest the praises of Israel." Man, once in the garden had, when surrounded by everything that testified of goodness and wisdom, dared to mistrust the holiness, and truth, and love of God. On the cross, when all around was dark and fearful, and full of wrath and terror and bitterness, yet could this holy one vindicate the hand that was thus stretched out in vengeance. And will the remembrance of this blessed perfect obedience ever pass away? No ; the very same Jesus has been raised up as God's high priest, ever to present before Him a full memorial of all the perfection of that service • on earth , and this memorial stands like the shewbread on the pure table, a perpetual record of the obedience of Him in whom alone the Israel of God are constituted righteous. The cakes were twelve, according to the number of the tribes, in order that each tribe might equally have its memorial presented before God on the holy table, of the same material, of the same weight, and of the same size. And so it is now respecting the Church of God. Some may, like Judah of old, have a more honoured and prominent position in the camp, or on the march; others, like Dan, be comparatively little esteemed, as being the hindmost of all the camps. And not only so — not only may the positions assigned to the servants of God on earth greatly differ, so that some may be fitted for a more prominent place of service than others ; but even as to the obedience and faithfulness of the saints, one may be far more diligent, and zealous, and true-hearted than another. If, however, we turn our eye away from the scene down here to the sanctuary above ; if we look at the memorial of accept- ance presented before God by Jesus for each in heaven, we shall find all there alike in blessing, and glory, and perfectness. The same perfect obedience is alike recorded on behalf of each; the same fragrance before God is presented for each. Dan, as much as Judab, had a cake of fine flour on -the table in God's presence. The weakest as well as the strongest, the unfaithful as well as the most faithful, the hindmost as well as foremost, stands in the same fulness of acceptance. " Righteous, because of the obedience of one," and "accepted in the beloved," are two great equalising truths of salvation, as much the blessing of each as of all believers in the Lord Jesus.

THE FRANKINCENSE

And thou shalt put pure frankincense upon each row, that it may be on the bread for a memorial, even an offering made by fire unto the Lord. — Lev. xxiv. 7. The Hebrew word *^^? 9 translated "frankincense? is derived from a root signifying " to be white ;" the word Lebanon is derived from the same root, so called because of its snow-clad summits ; and the Hebrew word for " the moon " is also from the same root, so called because of its silvery whiteness. This gum was, therefore, remarkable for its whiteness, and we also find in Exodus xxx. 34 the epithet "pure" - attached to it. The frankincense was a growth of earth as well as the fine flour; for in Cant. iv. 14, we read of " trees of frankincense;" and it seems to be added to the cakes upon the table, in order to express another aspect and truth respecting the Lord Jesus as man, namely, the purity and fragrance manifested by Him towards God in all His ways, actions, and thoughts. The purity of the ways and words of Jesus was not an affected sanctity, neither was it attained by separation from the haunts of men : it was not the mere result of habit, because observed by others, nor was its object the applause of men ; but it was the natural result of the spotlessness of His own nature. And it was ever before God He lived, and thought, and acted. If evil came from Satan or from man, even in that His comfort was to trace the will of God. In Him there were no mistrusts, no suspicions, as well as no murmurings of heart against God. His own character and ways were white and pure like the frankincense, and He knew the Father whom He so loved was good at all times and in all circumstances. All was open and transparent in Christ; He had nothing to conceal; He had no ambiguities, no double intentions, for He was single-eyed. His actions, therefore, and His words, were the transcript of Himself, the spontaneous exhibition of what He was intrinsically — all purity and fragrance. How wonderful, and yet how blessed, that a tree of earth should produce this sweet-smelling, pure frankincense! that a world, from whence sin and uncleanness and abomination had ceaselessly sent up an ill savour, should at length find one in its midst whost inmost thoughts as well as outward ways were pure and unsullied and fragrant like the frankincense before God ! What, therefore, the Lord intrinsically was as man typified by the fine flour, such also was He in all the pure and fragrant development of His character as represented by the frankincense ; and the eye and heart of God could rest on all this, and take delight in the beloved Son, ever well-pleasing to the Father, and who truly had the blessing of being " pure in heart," and was therefore fit to be under the eye of God.

THE SABBATH.

Every sabbath he shall set it in order before the Lord continually. — Lev. xxiv. 8. The seventh day was the first rest of God upon this earth ; but before it had run its course, sin had entered, and the rest of God here was effectually destroyed : from that moment creation began to send up a groan instead of a song of joy to God (Rom. viii. 22) ; and the sabbath has remained a melancholy memorial of a day never again to be known here — a day when once God looked on all the works of His hands and pronounced them very good, and could rest from all His work, and was refreshed. Any rest in this old creation is now hopeless: " this is not your rest, it is polluted," seems to be written on everything below; all decayeth and waxeth old and is ready to vanish away. He who well knew its former beauty — for His own hands had fashioned it— testified even on the sabbath-day, "my Father worketh hitherto and I work ;" for He found it all marred and ruined ; and man himself especially, the head and glory of it, so lost and degraded in body as well as spirit, that the only hope was that God would, out of the old, create something new, and would not cease to work until the former things should have passed away, and He could say, " Behold I make all things new." But though the rest has passed away from hence, yet in the sanctuary God has provided the memorial of a rest yet future. The record of a new creation has already been presented there before Him ; in the grace and purity and holiness of Jesus as the second man, the last Adam, the beginning of the new creation, already has God found perfect and eternal rest; and gladly can His eye now turn away from all that this earth has exhibited of its sin and ruin, to repose with blessed delight on all the perfectness and beauty of His Son, who has carried up a new joy, and new perfectness and beauty, into the mansions of glory. Thus, the presentation of fresh bread on the table every sabbath-day seems intended to connect thoughts of rest and joy with that ever fresh and blessed remembrance of the character and obedience of Christ, which He perpetually pre- sents before God on behalf of the Church ; a sure presage and foretaste of that new creation, into which sin, failure, and sorrow, shall never enter. Being taken from the children of Israel by an everlasting covenant. — Lev. xxiv. 8. One subject of interest and instruction respecting these types is the fact that all the various parts of the Tabernacle, as well as the sacrifices, were provided and presented by the people of Israel It seems to be the especial intention of God strongly to mark thereby their close identification with all those blessed things : so all belonged to them, though presented thus to Him ; and all was intended to be estimated and valued by them, though demanded and accepted by Him. They were types, not only of things themselves in the heavens, but also of the value and knowledge of, and communion with, those things, as estimated by the Israel of God below. The Church forms its estimate of Jesus through the Spirit; and that estimate will ever be according to God and be fragrant before Him. Another leading principle connected with the interpretation of these types seems to be, that where anything is in them made imperatively necessary, so that a heavy responsibility rested on Israel, or on Israel's priest of old, to perform it ; in the antitype all that has been fully and eternally answered by Christ, our great High Priest, so that the most stringent commands become the shadows of our highest and eternal blessings, secured by the faithfulness and power of Him who is a better one than Aaron. In the type now before us we have the loaves to be " taken from Israel by an everlasting covenant." The responsibility of this rested on Israel and its priesthood, and we know how all in consequence has utterly failed: but the blessing here prefigured cannot fail ; " the everlasting covenant " has been placed in the hands of one whose grace and power never can cease ; the love and faithfulness of our great High Priest are connected with a power and glory equal to the carrying out the purposes of God to their fullest extent. And He, whose priesthood is reckoned after another order than that of Aaron, ever presents for us that which is unceasing in its value and fragrance; an abiding memorial of perfectness, purity, and sweetness, on our behalf, secured by an everlasting covenant.

We find also the word "continual" applied to the bread. Though changed from week to week, yet it was ever the same bread in the presence of God. " And thou shalt set upon the table shewbread before me always" (Exod. xxv. 30); "before the Lord continually 1 ' (Lev. xxiv. 8); "the continual bread" (Num. iv. 7); "the continual shewbread " (2 Chron. ii. 4). Our souls know the value of that which ceases not in its power and efficacy towards God for us. With us all is changing; our thoughts, our actions, our resolves, vary from hour to hour. In the ways of God alone is continuance, and we shall be saved. (Isa. lxiv. 5.) His name Jehovah was revealed to Moses at the bush ; for as the " I AM " He was about to act towards Israel in redemption (a redemption of which He would not repent), and He was about to deal with His redeemed people in unchanging mercy, and with patient unvarying care, notwithstanding all their murmurings and evil that would be manifested in the way. And our High Priest, who claims the very name itself of Jehovah, with unwearied unwavering affection, retains for us His place of excellency before God, like the " continual " bread ever before Him, and presents for us now and ever the unfailing memorial of human perfectness and human obedience, in the full and blessed value of which we stand accepted before God.

And it shall he Aaron's and his sons' ; and they shall eat it in the holy place : for it is most holy unto him of the offerings of the Lord made by fire, by a perpetual statute. — Lev. xxiv. 9. All Israel, as the redeemed people of God, had food in common given to them from heaven ; the manna was daily supplied to them by God throughout their forty years' wanderings. Our Lord, as recorded in John vi., has we know alluded to this type, and there declared Himself to be the true bread from heaven ; and that life eternal is alone derived, and the sustainment of that life provided for, through eating His flesh and drinking His blood. Faith in Him as the lamb slain, the gift of God to a lost and ruined world, is life everlasting; and the soul that once has tasted this heavenly food lives on, forever sustained also by it. " Whoso eateth my flesh, and drinketh my blood, hath eternal life." " He that eateth me, even he shall live by me/' Moreover, to eat that flesh, and to drink that blood, is to abide in Christ in eternal, indissoluble union. " He that eateth my flesh, and drinketh my blood, abideth in me, and I in him." Here then is life, and life sustained, and life in union with the Son of man; and that through eating this bread from heaven. These are unchanging blessings, which pertain alike to every, even the feeblest, believer in the Lamb of God. But there was also in Israel food appropriated to the priesthood. They indeed, in common with the multitude, shared the daily supply from above; but besides this, they had the shewbread, as well as other offerings especially allotted to them. That which had been presented on the golden table before the Lord, which had been perpetually in His presence, and upon which His eye had for days rested with acceptance and delight, afterwards was partaken of by the priests in the holy place. Here we get a beautiful type of communion. Bread alike appreciated by God and by Israel's priests. A common subject of delight and refreshment. And this food ministered special strength to the priests for their service ; it was at hand for them in the very place of their ministry ; and the service in which they were engaged thus provided the suitable refreshment which they needed for their continued sustainment in it. The Scriptures tell us, for our joy, that we are partakers of the heavenly calling of our apostle and high priest, Jesus the Son of God; and that He hath made us unto our God kings and priests (Heb. iii. i ; Rev. i. 6 ; v. 10 ; i Pet. ii. 9) : we are, there- fore, of that royal priesthood which is to show forth the praises of Him that hath called us out of darkness into His marvellous light But how few of the Lord's people really desire to live, and act, and serve, according to this heavenly calling! How few occupy themselves about the holy things of God, so as to live as priests always in the precincts of the Tabernacle, and either serving, or ready to serve, in. the sanctuary! Generally speaking, the believer in Christ, if assured of his salvation, and having peace in his soul through faith in the blood of Christ, rests contented in that assur- ance, and desires little else than just to retain his present sense of peace and comfort of soul. Some, indeed, of the Lord's people have hardly advanced as far even as this ; and either set the sense of assurance of salvation at a distance afar off, esteeming it to be a matter of attainment only after long toiling and very varied experience ; or deem it presumptuous that any should be assured of present and eternal forgiveness, and question even the reality of that faith, which brings immediate peace to the soul. But surely, God in His mercy has not left us in doubt of the certainty of salvation, any more than He has left the question uncertain as to our complete and eternal ruin by nature. If He has unequivocally declared the desperate condition of the disease, He has also declared the certain and immediate efficacy of the remedy. And surely also He has not made His children to be a royal priesthood, without giving them a holy and happy sphere for the exercise of that priesthood, and directions and a capacity for serving Him according to their heavenly calling. It is written, " How much more shall the blood of Christ, who through the eternal Spirit offered Himself without spot to God, purge your conscience from dead works to serve the living God?" (Heb. ix. 14.) And God has left His redeemed people in this world for a while, not that their salvation may be made more secure — for that were impossible — but that they may occupy themselves in His truth and in His service, and may know the things that have been freely given to them of Him. Priestly service of old was of very varied kinds. The priests had not only to offer gifts and sacrifices, to put incense before God, and whole burnt-offerings on the altar, but they had also to teach Israel God's judgments and His law. They had to put difference between holy and unholy, between unclean and clean; to discern leprosy and all the varied forms of defilement; to cleanse and to cut off— to restore and to put without the camp. As priests, therefore (of whom Israel's priests were but a type), the Church of God has a vast and varied field of labour and service- To appreciate and understand the sacrifice, to know how to use and testify to its value and sweet savour, both for the blessing of their own souls and that of others ; to worship, to pray, and praise ; all these happy exercises of their priestly calling appertain to the saints of God. But besides this, we have as priests to know the world as to its defilements and uncleannesses, and the flesh as to its corruptions and lusts ; its contacts of sin and death, its subtle workings and open rebellions ; and if in seeking to serve God we find ourselves weak and fainting ; if we are made more deeply acquainted with His holiness, and our own worthlessness and corruption ; if our souls get pressed down under a sense of incompetence and evil, when weighing our actions in the balance of the sanctuary, and we feel how incessantly all our service,' all our endeavours at obedience, are mingled with imperfection and failure — then let us remember that God has provided special food for our sustainment in these circumstances ; and that we may, through the rich provision of His mercy, turn and feed on Him, whose unleavened purity and fragrance is our strength and blessing, and whose flesh we shall ever find to be 'meat indeed, and whose blood to be drink indeed, for the sustainment and comfort and reassurance of our hearts before God.

One who seeks to serve God will find that the very service will bring him into new scenes of difficulty and trial; will discover to him weaknesses and corruptions in himself of which he would otherwise be little, if at all, aware. And God has graciously provided that such as desire thus to exercise themselves as His priests, shall have blessed communion with Him respecting the person and ways of His Son, whereby they may be strengthened and encouraged still to persevere, and be more and more fitted for the various exercises of soul into which they may be led. And whilst they get a deeper insight into the flesh and its evil, whilst they discover more and more its miserable inconsistencies, its secret envy, pride, vanity, and self- esteem, they can turn from this loathsome picture to feed on that which is pure and holy, and which will sanctify the inward motives and affections, at the same time that it strengthens and refreshes. Christ known and fed upon as the unleavened one, according to the perfectness and fragrant grace of His human character, will be food, distasteful indeed to the natural man, but invigorating and blessed to the inner man; and in the very act of thus feeding the soul will be conformed more and more to His likeness. May we relish this heavenly food; may the tempting baits and allurements of the flesh fail before it; may we hunger and thirst more after it, and find our desire after it increased by seeking to occupy ourselves in those things which pertain to us as priests, consecrated to God through the precious blood of Him " who loved us and gave Himself for us !"

THE CROWNS AND BORDER.

Exod. xxv. 24, 25. — And make thereto a crown of gold round about. And thou shalt make unto it a border of a handbreadth round about, and thou shalt make a golden crown to the border thereof round about.

Exod. xxxvii. 11, 12. — And he made there- unto a crown of gold round about. Also, he made thereunto a border of a hand- breadth round about; and made a crown of gold for the border thereof round about.

Around the table on which the cakes were disposed, a crown was to be fixed; and a ledge also extended the dimensions of the table by a handbreadth, around which was attached another crown of gold. The same word is here used for "crown" as was noticed before respecting the Ark; a rim or binding formed an upright ledge round the table, and another rim formed a ledge round the border. The object of this first crown was, it would appear, to retain the bread securely in its position on the table, so that it might not get displaced, during the progress of the journey, through any failures in the Kohathites who carried the table on their shoulders. We have here again an intimation of the secure and lasting provision made for the continuance of those blessings which depend on the priestly office of Christ. " To be in the presence of God for us," is not an occasional interrupted service of our High Priest, but at all times we may confidently say, " Now in the presence of God for us," like the shewbread (or presence-bread, as it might be termed) always retained by the golden circle on the pure table before the Lord. Not only is the Mercy Seat, the place of grace, securely retained in its appointed place by the goldencrown, but there is the same height of perfectness, the same fragrance of

Christ ever under the eye of God on our behalf, unchanged by any feebleness, failings, or wan- derings of His people below. The use of the border or shelf added to the table was, it seems, to form a place of support for the golden vessels attached to the Shewbread Table, whereon they probably were placed during the journeys. In Exod. xxxvii. 16, the vessels are spoken of as "on the table;" and in Num. iv. 7, where directions are given for carry- ing the table, these vessels are directed to be placed upon it. The direction also respecting the place of the rings into which the staves were inserted for carrying the table, is that they shall be "over against the border." (Exod. xxv. 27.) This would seem to intimate that the border was a part of the table which had reference to its being borne by the staves on the march. It is probable, therefore, that this border was intended for the place of the golden vessels during the wanderings of the people of Israel in the wilderness. The object of the crown or ledge attached to the border would then be to render the vessels secure in their position when carried on the table. We are here reminded of a careful and diligent foresight on the part of our God, to secure and maintain unshaken all our blessings in Christ. Ages of declension have rolled on, and yet not one golden vessel of the sanctuary has been disturbed, not one ministry of our great High Priest, whether manifestly important, or apparently trivial, has ceased. Because He is God unchanging in His purpose, and unwearied in his gracious service, therefore we are not cut off ; and at the close not one good thing shall be found to have failed of all that He hath spoken respect- ing us. We feel the absolute need of being committed to the care and keeping of one who has (as it were) the enduring power and unchangeableness of the gold, whilst his sympathies and feelings as a man link Him on with His suffering people on earth ; and we scarcely know which most to appreciate, the wisdom and power and glory of Him who stands before God for us, or the gentleness and grace with which He who knows our infirmities can sympathize and assist us in all our need.

The staves attached to the table indicate, as in the case of the Ark, a provision for the moving and carrying this holy vessel with Israel during their march; and so, throughout our journey here, God has provided us with living bread for the sustain- ment and strength of our souls; and our fellowship with Him need not be interfered with, or interrupted, whatever be the appointed path we have to tread; but "pleasant bread" placed on His own table is ever presented to us by Him, and blessings result- ing from happy communion with the Father respecting His Son Jesus Christ may be fully and richly known even in the midst of the turmoil and weariness of the wilderness journey.

THE VESSELS ATTACHED TO THE TABLE OF SHEWBREAD. *

Exod. xxv. 29. — And thou shalt make the Exod. xxxvii. 16. — And he made the vessels dishes thereof, and spoons thereof, and covers which were upon the table, his dishes and his thereof, and bowk thereof, to pour out withal ; spoons, and his bowls, and his covers to pour of pure gold shalt thou make them. out withal, of pure gold. Here are four distinct sets of golden vessels attached to the Shewbread Table, and placed upon it, when the table was carried ; let us briefly enter upon their uses.

THE DISHES.

First as to the dishes. The Hebrew word ninpp, here translated "dishes," only occurs again in Scripture in Num. vii. : throughout that chapter it is translated " chargers/' which were silver vessels filled with fine flour for a meat-offering, part of the offerings of the princes at the dedication of the altar. Our word dish might have been fitly retained in both places; for it is the ordinary word expressive of a vessel for holding food. Here we find golden dishes attached to the table: the use of them may be conjectured to be for the sustaining the bread before the priests, for their eating, whilst they placed fresh bread on the table. The dishes would stand around the table on the six days of the week, as a memorial to the priests that the very bread then on the table before the Lord, was on the seventh day to be their food; and when they did partake of the shewbread, the golden dishes would bear it up before them, at the same time that the pure table presented fresh bread to God. And may not this draw our minds to a truth we often have practically to realize, namely, that we need not only a supply of spiritual food for the strength and refresh- ment of our souls, but also that He who supplies it should be as the dish to present and sustain it before our souls? We need not only subjects of communion, but also to have those subjects kept before us, and immediately presented to us by our great High Priest Our helplessness is such that we are dependent on one who shall place the fitting food even before our eyes and in our very hands : often have we to say, " Feed me with food convenient for me," food in due season. And Jesus is the one whom God has consecrated to be as the golden dish, sustaining before us its heavenly food; to invite our taste, and supply that which may strengthen us to serve God; and whilst thus feeding on Him as presented to us by Himself, we have true fellow- ship with the Father, who delights and rejoices in the same fragrant food, and rests in us as presented to Him in the spotless one, ever in His presence for us. The golden dishes thus typically linked on the priests who ministered in the holy place with the golden table, were silent tokens that there was food in those heavenly courts which could be eaten in holy fellowship with the Lord Himself. How blessed the experience of that soul who can say with the apostle John, " That which was from the beginning, which we have heard, which we have seen with our eyes, which we have looked upon, and our hands have hamiled of the Word of Life V What a real and individual thing is communion with the Father and the Son ! One cannot have it for another, as one cannot eat to sustain another. It is not mere knowledge of truth, or acquaintance with all doctrine or mysteries ; but it is the tasting, the handling for oneself, the appropriating to oneself, the WORD OF LIFE. It is a joy with which the stranger inter-meddleth not.

THE SPOONS.

The spoons (in Hebrew HIS?) were small hollow vessels of gold, holding, as the Hebrew word seems to denote, about a handful. From Num. vii. we learn that twelve golden spoons were presented by the princes, filled with incense, for the use of the sanctuary.

Hence the use of these spoons was to hold incense; and the word OviaKas, the Septuagint name for the same vessels, denotes that they were considered to be used for incense. 4 The question immediately arises, why should spoons holding incense be needed at the Table of Shewbread? In answer to this it may be observed, that we shall find, if we carefully read the types of the Tabernacle and its service, that there is a studied purpose of the Spirit of God to link together various offices, various services and vessels, so that they might be contemplated, not only as they stand in distinctness or contrast one from the other, but as all combining together, and forming a beautiful chain, dependent one on the other, and portraying, as a whole, a blended picture of heavenly ministry. One great difficulty we find in learning truth is to combine; and the types seem written to teach us this amongst other things ; so that whilst they present varied and often contrasted aspects of the Lord, yet we have to connect and mingle them together, so as to hold them, or the truths they teach, not antagonistically, but as forming a perfect harmonious whole ; we have to learn to unite and not to sever. Those who are accustomed to meditating on the offerings in Leviticus are well aware of this fact For example, the burnt- offering and the sin-offering stand broadly contrasted with each other, the one being all consumed in fragrant acceptance, the other burnt as under wrath outside the camp : and yet in many respects the sin-offering approaches the burnt-offering, part of it being burnt on the altar of acceptance, whilst in the burnt-offering itself, atone- ment for sin is involved. So again we find the meat-offering, though having a distinct aspect of its own, yet always combined at the altar with the burnt-offering; and on certain great occasions the whole round of offerings were presented together before the Lord. So, it is believed to be also respecting the various holy vessels of the Tabernacle. Though each had its distinct use, and each can be contemplated by itself, yet in every great act of priestly service all were linked together, and were in active operation at the same time ; and the smaller golden vessels which we find attached to the Shewbread Table and Candlestick were these links, uniting together in one ministration the several vessels of the Sanctuary, and forming thereby a golden chain of blessed service, all occupied, all presented, all rendering at the same moment, in the presence of God, their full value on behalf of Israel.

To turn then to the incense spoons. In the enumeration of the various vessels of the Sanctuary we shall find none specified for holding incense except these; when, therefore, the High Priest had to put incense on the golden altar, he would have to go to the Table of Shewbread to fetch the spoonful from thence. In this act he would link, as it were, these two vessels, the altar and the table together ; he would remember, whilst he sent up a cloud of fragrance from the burning coals on the altar, to cover any ill savour that might have been exhibited by Israel, that at the same moment the perpetual bread presented, on the golden table, an unchanged aspect of perfectness on their behalf ; and thus, whilst defect had by the one vessel to be met and covered over, perfectness was on the other still preserved unaltered under the gaze of the Lord. And does not this afford a true type of the ministra- tion of our High Priest? Because He ever liveth to make intercession for us (like the incense altar with its fragrant cloud), does He cease at the same time to present the full aspect of perfectness on our behalf, as typified by the shew- bread? In a word, is not His power to combine the presentation of ail per- fection with the covering over of all imperfection, one great blessing of His priest- hood? Whilst therefore the truth respecting our weak and failing condition below is never forgotten, but is provided for in His ceaseless intercession, at the same time a standing is retained for us above, beyond all failure and all weakness. The priest who lights the incense altar has his thoughts full of the remembrance of the pure table and its twelve presence loaves, from whence he has taken the golden spoon full of the perfume.

THE BOWLS AND CUPS

The two remaining sets of vessels attached to the table were " bowls and cups," and the use to which they were applied is immediately seen from the words which follow, "to pour out withal and Num. iv. 7, "the drink-offering/' bowls and cups. Here the same question occurs as before, to what end were libation vessels kept at the Table of Shewbread. This will be satisfactorily solved by a reference to Num. xxviii. 7, where the command is given to " pour out the strong wine unto the Lord for a drink-offering, in the holy place" This chapter is one of fresh directions to Israel respecting their principal offerings, and seems to confine the pouring out of the drink-offerings in the holy place to certain special occasions. The word trans- lated strong wine y "1?^, only occurs in this place as connected with the drink-ofter- ings ; and the principle of the precept seems to be, that Israel's daily drink-offerings, and also those offered on their great feast days, were to be poured out in the holy place ; 6 that is, inside the Tabernacle. The ordinary place for pouring out the wine was probably the brazen altar; for the worship of an individual Israelite did not extend beyond that place. In Exod. xxx. 9, we find a precept forbidding a drink- offering to be poured on the golden altar of incense ; from which we may infer that it was the custom to do so on the other altar, where the meat-offering was always offered. In ordinary cases an Israelite brought his burnt-offering, with the meat- offering and drink-offering connected with it, to the altar of burnt-offering, and all was presented and offered there ; but when all Israel presented their corporate offerings, as was the case morning and evening w r hen the daily lamb was offered, and also on the sabbaths, and new moons, and appointed feasts, then the accom- panying drink-offerings were poured out in the holy place, and not at the brazen altar. And this is in accordance with Israel's corporate standing ; for though individually none but a priest could enter the holy place, yet corporately they were regarded as having access to the inner courts, as is intimated by the fact of the princes presenting golden spoons of incense, which could only be used at the incense altar ; and still more distinctly is it proved from Lev. iv., where the sin of the whole con- gregation is represented as so penetrating into the Tabernacle, that the blood of atonement had to be sprinkled before the vail and upon the incense altar just as much as if an anointed priest had sinned. It is concluded therefore, that as the drink-offerings of Israel corporately had to be poured out within the Tabernacle, and as all the service of the Sanctuary carried on there was conducted in golden vessels, these bowls and cups were kept for the purpose of pouring out the wine before the Lord whenever a drink-offering was presented by the whole congregation. These vessels were of two sizes, perhaps on account of the different measures of wine directed to be poured out. There were in like manner two sizes of silver bowls for meat-offerings, presented by the princes. (Num. vii.)

Here again these libation vessels seem to have been links uniting the service of the altar of burnt-offering outside, with the vessels and service within the Sanc- tuary. So that when the sweet savour of the daily burnt-offering lamb ascended from the outer court unto heaven, and Israel began and ended the day under the shelter and acceptance of that all-fragrant sacrifice ; at the same time the priest poured out in the holy place the full and rich libation of wine near the pure table ; expressive of the truth, that whilst the remembrance of the lamb in all its perfectness, presented unto God in death, was an offering of a sweet smelling savour, grateful and fragrant to Jehovah, a full measure also of new joy was ministered unto Him in heaven ; a joy derived not from creation, but from redemption, the result of that one offering presented to God from the earth. When the foundations of the earth were laid, " the morning stars sang together, and all the sons of God had shouted for joy and He who had made all things very good, rested and was refreshed by the works of His own hands ; but that joy had all along since passed away. An universal groan suc- ceeded the shout and song of creation; labour succeeded rest; till at length HE came whose delight it was to do the will of God. On Him the Spirit of God could for the first time on earth descend and abide, and through His service and work in life and death, a new and lasting joy, like the strong wine of the drink-offering, was ministered to the heart of God; a joy, in the anticipation of which Jesus Himself had been strengthened to endure the cross, and despise the shame. And when at length that Holy One poured out His life on the cross, then was this new and blessed joy tasted by God. He had been glorified on the earth, His will had been perfectly fulfilled, the work He had appointed to be done had been finished, every word of His had been accomplished ; and now He could rejoice in the new and eternal work of redemption, which would not fail as creation had failed before, but which would forever minister lasting and strong joy ; the eternal record of the wisdom and love of His heart who had planned, and the grace and love and obedience of Him who had executed it. And now as each poor sinner hails the blessed message of salva- tion, and turns in faith and hope to rest on the slain lamb, a fresh bowl, as it were, of the strong wine is again poured out in the Sanctuary, the value of the lamb slain is again told out in joy in the presence of God ; the flowing drink-offering brought from the burning altar bids, again and again, the song arise in the heavenly courts above : — " Verily, I say unto you, there is joy in the presence of the angels of God over one sinner that repenteth." " It is meet that we should make merry and be glad." We have in i Sam. xxi. a striking and instructive scene connected with the shew- bread, and which, as it is alluded to by the blessed Lord Himself, it may be profit- able to pause for a little and consider. The Lord Jesus uses this account of David eating the shewbread to illustrate one of the most blessed principles in the heart of God, " I will have mercy and not sacrifice and David seems to have apprehended this truth, and to have acted on it on this occasion ; for he was a man after God's own heart, and could read and appreciate the deep and ceaseless love of God. He knew that everything must give way to grace, which was the ruling principle in the heart of Him with whom he had to do ; so that the law itself, with its stringent pre- cepts, must bow before it ; and the necessity of one of God's saints was plea enough to set aside its prescribed ritual. How bold, how daring is faith, and how varied in its exercise. Jonathan in the energy and power of it could climb the garrisoned fort of the Philistines and beat them down before him; David could in the confidence of like precious faith take the hallowed bread and eat and distribute to his hungry followers. Both alike trusted in the grace and power of a living God and knew His mind and ways. But whilst this eating of the shewbread exhibits to us the con- fidence of David in the grace and pity of his God, at the same time we see by his other actions in this scene, that he is sadly wanting in his trust in the same God for present help and safety in the midst of his difficulties. He first dissembles with Ahimelech; subsequently, even whilst the holy bread is in his mouth, he asks for a weapon of defence. There is none for him there but the vanquished sword of Goliath ; for the Tabernacle of God provides no fleshly weapons, and the sword of the Philistine was there harmlessly suspended behind the ephod, not as a weapon for use, but as a trophy only of one of the Lord's victories over the flesh. But David eagerly accepts that; " There is none like that, give it me." What a contrast here with the faith of the stripling, who in the valley of Elah had found the sword of the giant powerless against the name of the Lord of hosts. There, in the energy and spring-time of his faith, having before proved the faithfulness and power of God in secret, he came forth into open conflict, undaunted at the vastness of the foe, and measuring the mighty power that was thus opposed to him by a greater and mightier name, the name of the living God. His eye of faith saw the Lord of Hosts as the combatant on the one side, and but uncircumcised flesh as the opponent on the other; and a pebble from a brook was a weapon sufficient to decide such a conflict. But the early first love of David seems subsequently to have become deadened by the series of trials he had endured at the hands of Saul. Had it been still the Philistine, it may be he could have borne it and conquered ; or had it been again a lion and a bear, he would have slain them : but trial of a different kind had come upon him : he found a foe now in the Lord's anointed ; one whom he had esteemed his friend and benefactor had now proved his unrelenting enemy. The circumstances of his life also had changed. The unobtrusive path of faith, alone with God, where lie had first as the shepherd boy relied on, and proved the strength of Jehovah's arm, had been exchanged for a conspicuous place of honour in the palace of Saul : it may be even the sweet friendship of Jonathan had a little intruded upon the place the Lord once held in his heart ; and now, obliged to flee, and hunted as a partridge upon the mountains, his trust in the living God waxes feeble, and he fails to realise, as once he had done, the present help of Jehovah in trouble. Then to what can he turn but to his own resources, Dissimulation, and the very weapon of the flesh, the sword of Goliath, become the sources of his confidence ; and he who had once, in the simple confidence of his faith in God, refused the armour of Saul as a mere encumbrance, now resorts to the weapon of a vanquished foe ; and, as if he had proved it, says, "There is nothing like that, give it me." And yet he had a heart in the main true to God, and able, in the midst of all this declension, to hold fast his knowledge of God's grace, so as even to say of the hallowed bread, that it was " in a manner common, yea, though it were sanctified this day in the vessel." May not this read us an instructive lesson as to the difference between that abiding, practical faith and dependence on the Lord, which knows and trusts in Him as the living God, and that faith in Him as the God of all grace and the God of salvation, which may still remain in the heart, even when through declension, or other causes, there is but little present confidence in Him for help or deliverance in difficulty or danger. And what a sad spectacle does David present with the sword of Goliath this second time in his hand! The giant himself, armed with his own weapons, had once inspired terror, and had

presented a front of greatness and power, before which the natural man might well have quailed. But the man of God, attempting to manage the weapons of the flesh, affords but a spectacle of derision to the enemy. The sword he tried to wield was unsuited to his power ; he must have felt like a culprit in its very use ; the song of his former triumphs sounded like a knell of defeat in his ears, and he got out of the scene only through a stratagem of weakness and idiotcy, which rendered him so despicable in the sight of his foes, that he is allowed to depart as a useless madman. And so, it must ever be with the man of God. Either God is everything to him, or the flesh and its weapons will be resorted to. If the living God is not the resource of the soul in every trial and on every occasion, worldly policy and human expedients and plans will take His place ; and then the child of God, instead of winning victories of faith, and triumphing in the strength of the Lord, sinks down lower even than the level of the world around him, and becomes a mere object of ridicule or pity. And yet in the midst of all this there will be gleams, as it were, of faith, which will still manifest that the mercy and grace of God are, after all, known and prized as the real stay and rest of the soul. This humbling lesson was not without its blessed results to David. The thirty-fourth Psalm tells us how his soul had again been restored to its entire confidence in God ; the cave Adullam is a more healthful place for his soul than the palace of Saul ; and the distressed and needy wanderers that gather round him were less likely, it may be, to divert his heart from the Lord, than Jonathan with his sweet and lasting friendship. And this Psalm tells us of David's renewed trust in God, not only as the God " who would have mercy rather than sacrifice," but as the one who would uphold, and help, and deliver, and who would not surfer them that seek Him to want any good thing. Instead of there being nothing like the sword of Goliath, it now is, " My soul shall make her boast in the Lord." In the Temple there were ten Tables of Shewbread (2 Chron. iv. 8, 19), which were made, as it would appear, entirely of gold. (1 Chron. xxviii. 16.) May not the increased number of tables, thus presented before God in the Sanctuary, point to the time yet to come, when the value of Jesus shall be appreciated on earth by whole nations, in contrast with the present dispensation, when those who own Him are but few, ten being often used in Scripture to express an unlimited number.

We read of the Shewbread Table only on two other occasions: (2 Chron. xxix. 18) — when the Priests and Levites, at the instigation of Hezekiah, restored the worship of the Lord, cleansing the Temple, Altar, and Table of Shewbread with its vessels; and lastly (Neh. x. 33), when, after the return from the captivity, provision was made for a constant supply of shewbread, and for the other continual offerings of the Sanctuary. It may be an interesting subject of inquiry, whether the Altar of Wood, mentioned in Ezek. xli. 22, and called "the table that is before the Lord," has any reference to the Shewbread Table; and, if so, whether it may not be a vessel combining table and altar in one.

NOTES TO THE TABLE OF SHEWBREAD.
THE COMPARATIVE SIZES OF THE VESSELS.

The Ark

The Table of Shewbread .

The Altar of Incense

The Altar of Burnt-offering

The Holy Vessels and Furniture of the Tabernacle of Israel

LENGTH.

Cubits.

2
I
5

BREADTH.

Cubits.

«i

I

I

5

HEIGHT.
Cubits.
U
U
2

3

* The word "pure" HDT applied to the frankincense, is different from the word "pure" often used respecting the gold and some of the vessels of the Sanctuary. The latter word seems to mean

intrinsic purity of nature, as contrasted with uncleanness of nature ; so that this latter is the word used to designate beasts that are "clean." The former word attached to the frankincense seems used to indicate a purity practically developed and manifested. He, therefore, that was " tahore" pure like the gold by nature, was also "zachar," pure like the frankincense in his ways.

In the usual drawings of the Shewbread Table, the cakes are arranged in two heaps, piled one upon the other at each end of the table. An entirely different arrangement has (it will be perceived) been adopted in the drawings which accompany this exposition : the reason for thus departing from the traditional arrangement of the table is, that the express declaration in the word is that the cakes were to be "set in two rows, six on a row, upon the pure table," and not in two piles or heaps. Moreover, the bread is called, "bread of faces," literally; which seems also to imply that the cakes were spread out on the table so as to present their "faces," as it were, towards the eye of God ; and in Exod. xl. 23, Moses is said to have "set the bread in order upon the table before the Lord," an expression which also would appear to indicate an arrangement of the bread on the table in two rows. It will be perceived from the drawings that the frankincense has been represented as strewed over the tops of the loaves, so as to give them a white appearance, and not placed in cups, as generally represented ; this has also been done as seemingly more in accordance with the direct language of Scripture. "And thou shalt put pure frankincense upon each row, that it may be on the bread for a memorial." The thought has suggested itself to the Author, whether the modern practice of "frosting" cakes, used on certain special occasions, such as marriage, etc., may not have arisen from some tradition respecting the white aspect of the holy loaves of shewbread thus covered with frankincense. If so, how would this afford another instance of the way in which men have perverted the truths of God, to feed their own corrupt lusts and imaginations.

Incense has to be distinguished from frankincense: the former was composed of four fragrant gums, whereas frankincense was a sweet white gum of itself. Incense was burnt in the holy and most holy places frankincense was only burnt at the brazen altar outside. Nowhere are spoons spoken of as holding frankincense, so that it is not apprehended that these spoons were for holding the frankincense on the bread. It is true that in the Arch of Titus, two small vessels, like cups, are represented standing on a kind of table, which by many is supposed to be a representation of the Table of Shewbread; but it seems very doubtful whether it be in fact intended for the Shewbread Table. The proportions do not at all agree with those of the table in Exodus. And even supposing the sculptor was accurate in his delineations of the spoils taken by Titus, yet the vessels of the Temple then were not the original ones of the Tabernacle, or of Solomon's Temple ; and tradition had long exercised its baneful effects over the Jews, so that we have only to read Josephus, and to compare some of his narratives with the Scriptures, to be convinced of his utter disregard of the plain language of truth before him, and how unworthy of credit any uninspired person is when he attempts to deal with the things of God. This subject will be again alluded to under "The Candlestick."

The word Tfiffi), translated "covers," occurs again in I Chron. xxviii. 17, where it is rendered "cups;" and this is manifestly the correct translation, because the words "to pour out withal" are, in Exod. xxxvii. 16, connected with these vessels. They, as well as the bowls, were used as libation vessels, the same phrase, "to pour out withal," being connected indiscriminately with the cups as well as bowls. It would seem as if the translators were at a loss to know what the use of libation vessels could be at the Shewbread Table, and therefore altered the ordinary- translation, "to pour out," into "to cover." The margin, however, retains the right rendering. In Num. iv. 7, where the vessels of the table are again enumerated, "the cups" are called in the Hebrew " the drink-offering cups," which renders the use of these vessels still more evident.

* There are two ways in which "the holy place" is expressed in Hebrew, 8F3j3n and KHfJ DpQ. The former is used generally where the covered Tabernacle is meant, and is translated in English with the word place in Italics, "the holy place ;" the latter is more general, and includes all the precincts of the Tabernacle with its outer court, and is translated "the holy place," the word "place" not being in italics. It might, perhaps, be better translated by "a holy place." This will be proved correct as a general rule, but there are a few exceptions.

May not this be the reason why, in Num. iv. 7, the cups and bowls are called ^|£)}n, " the drink-offering ;" as if to denote their especial connection with THE great drink-offering, that is, the one presented by all the people.

THE CANDLESTICK

Exod. xxv. 31-36. — And thou shalt make a candlestick of pure gold : of beaten work shall the candlestick be made : his shaft, and his branches, his bowls, his knops, and his flowers, shall be of the same. And six branches shall come out of the sides of it ; three branches of the candlestick out of the one side, and three branches of the candlestick out of the other side : three bowls made like unto almonds, with a knop and a flower in one branch ; and three bowls made like almonds in the other branch, with a knop and a flower : so in the six branches that come out of the candlestick. And in the candlestick shall be four bowls made like unto almonds, with their knops and their flowers. And there shall be a knop under two branches of the same, and a knop under two branches of the same, and a knop under two branches of the same, according to the six branches that proceed out of the candle- stick. Their knops and their branches shall be of the same: all of it shall be one beaten work of pure gold.

Exod. xxxvii. 17-22. — And he made the candlestick of pure gold : of beaten work made he the candlestick ; his shaft, and his branch, his bowls, his knops, and his flowers, were of the same : and six branches going out of the sides thereof ; three branches of the candlestick out of the one side thereof, and three branches of the candlestick out of the other side thereof : three bowls made after the fashion of almonds in one branch, a knop and a flower ; and three bowls made like almonds in another branch, a knop and a flower : so throughout the six branches going out of the candlestick. And in the candlestick were four bowls made like almonds, his knops, and his flowers : and a knop under two branches of the same, and a knop under two branches of the same, and a knop under two branches of the same, according to the six branches going out of it. Their knops and their branches were of the same: all of it was one beaten work of pure gold.

WE are familiar with the use of "light* in Scripture as expressive of the nature and manifested character of God, and of the Lord Jesus. " God is light, and in Him is no darkness at all." (1 John i. 5.) "That was the true light, which lighteth every man that cometh into the world." (John i. 9.) " I am the light of the world." (John viii. 12, &c.) Life also is an inseparable attendant upon light, and light is intimately connected with life. " In Him was life, and the life was the light of men." (John i. 4.) " He that followeth me shall not walk in darkness but shall have the light of life." (John viii, 12.) "To be enlightened with the light of the living." (Job xxxiii. 30.) Christ arose from the dead, the source and sustainer of the Church in life and light ; so that it is written of believers, that they have been " quickened together with Christ, and have been raised up together, and made to sit together in heavenly places in Him" (Eph. ii. 5, 6); and, "your life is hid with Christ in God: when Christ, who is our life, shall appear, then shall ye also appear with Him in glory" (Col iii. 3, 4); and, "ye were sometimes darkness, but now are ye light in the Lord" (Eph. v. 8.) The resurrection of Christ was the first moment of the life of the Church, for it was quickened and raised up together with Him ; in blessed and eternal union with Him is that life maintained ; and He, thus " raised far above all principality, and power, and might, and dominion, and every name that is named, not only in this world, but also in that which is to come," is ever the spring and source of all its glory and joy. The Candlestick of gold seems to shadow forth this wondrous mystery: in it we find a type of union, a truth scarcely to be found elsewhere foreshadowed in the whole Mosaic ritual. It was the most elaborate of all the vessels of the Sanctuary as to its workmanship, being richly ornamented ; the other vessels were studiously plain ; it was of " beaten work" (^^i?P) ; a word which conveys the idea of solidity, as well as of being wrought by hand, instead of cast in a mould. The workman who had thus to fashion such a richly chased vessel must have pondered minutely over every part, and must have bestowed intense labour and skill alike on every portion ; his tool must have been guided with careful and unerring precision, so as to form the delicate flowers that adorned it ; and yet the pattern and symmetry of the whole must have rested in his mind, whilst from the one solid mass of gold he beat out every part. Does not this afford us an apt illustration of that skill and marvellous wisdom of God, displayed in Christ and the Church, as fashioned by Him, and quickened together out of the grave — the elaborate result of His deep and eternal counsels, the great and abiding manifestation of His manifold wisdom, and of the exceeding riches of his grace? (Eph. ii. 7; iii. 10.) The place of death was that selected by God as the laboratory out of which to display His mighty power and skill ; there in secret was the body and its members curiously wrought ; from thence was the new and perfect man raised up in beauty and glory. " I will praise thee; for I am fearfully and wonderfully made: marvellous are thy works, and that my soul knoweth right well. My substance was not hid from thee, when I was made in secret, and curiously wrought in the lowest parts of the earth. Thine eyes did 'see my substance yet being unperfect; and in thy book all my members were written, which in continuance were fashioned, when as yet there was none of them." (Psalm cxxxix. 14-16.)

THE SHAFT AND ITS BRANCH.

If we accurately read the portion of Scripture descriptive of the Candlestick, we shall find that the central part of the vessel, consisting of a shaft and its branch, is that which, apart from the rest, is eminently called " the Candlestick." It should be observed that in our translation, there is an error in Exod. xxv. 31, where "his branches" should have been "his branch," not plural, but singular, which is corrected in Exod. xxxvii. 17, where it is rightly rendered "his branch." The shaft, or main stem, of the vessel was of beaten gold, as well as the most delicate flower that adorned it (Num. viii. 4): the skill of the artificer was as much seen in thus forming the solid support of the whole, as in the minutest details of its most costly ornaments. From the sides of this shaft proceeded six branches, three out of the one side, and three out of the other. This presents to us a type of Christ Himself, as the source from whence the Church proceeds, as well as its eternal support, and in whom it abides in indissoluble union. The word "shaft" is significant, being the same that is rendered "thigh" in the margin of

Gen. xlvL 26; Exod. L 5; Jud. viii. 30. As the children are represented in those passages as proceeding from the thigh, or loins of their parent, so the six branches spring from, and are dependent on, the shaft of the Candlestick. And thus Christ is the pillar of support and life of the Church; all rest on Him, all proceed from Him: His life, His strength, His firmness, His glory and beauty are theirs. In blessed dependence on Him, and owing its existence to Him, the Church abides unchangeably united to its glorious head ; one life pervades it all, one spirit flows through all its members, one glory and beauty is alike the portion of every part ; and yet all is traced up to its centre and its source — Christ, " in whom it is all fitly framed together," and from whom it all proceeds. And the wise artificer has wrought this central stem of solid beaten gold; firmness and stability are its chief characteristics.

But the Candlestick had not only its shaft, but also " its branch;" the main stem sprung up almost imperceptibly into a central branch, adorned with its buds, blossoms, and fruit. There was this distinction between this and the other six branches of the Candlestick, namely, that this sprung up from the central shaft, they proceeded out of the sides ; and also this was more profusely adorned than the others, and rose to a greater height, towering above them. For we shall find from the text that there were three bowls, a knop and a flower only in each of the six branches ; whilst in the Candlestick, or central portion, there were four bowls, their knops, and their flowers : that is, there were four of each kind of ornaments. This central part was therefore more adornedand would in consequence rise to a greater height than the side branches, though of the same fashion with them, and formed out of the same mass of beaten gold. 1 Here we have another aspect of truth presented to us in type respecting the blessed Lord, as Himself head of that body of which He is the origin ; and taking His place in the Church, as one in the midst of His fellows, at the same time that He is as the shaft or pillar on which it all depends. It is written, " He that sanctifieth and they who are sanctified are all of one : for which cause He is not ashamed to call them brethren ; saying, I will declare thy name unto my brethren ; in the midst of the

Church will I sing praise unto thee. And again, Behold I and the children which God hath given me." (Heb. ii. 11-13.) Thus He is a branch in the midst of the branches; yet ever more glorious and lofty than they, for in all things He hath the pre-eminence. In the midst of His fellows yet anointed with the oil of gladness above them. (Psalm xlv. 7.) A man in the midst of men, yet "fairer than the children of men f "the chiefest among ten thousand; ' "the altogether lovely." There is oneness, and yet pre-eminence; similarity, and yet superiority.

THE BOWLS LIKE ALMONDS.

There were three sets of ornaments in this beautiful vessel, bowls or cups like almonds, knops, and flowers. As to the first, the bowls like almonds, we have an analogy in the fruit yielded by Aaron's rod, which were almonds. This rod has been previously referred to as a beautiful type of the risen Christ, so that it will not be necessary again to enter upon it It may, however, be remarked, that the almond is selected here, and for Aaron's rod, probably because it is the first tree to awake from the sleep of winter, and is therefore an appropriate type of Him who is " the first- fruits of them that slept." Its early vigour heralds the approach of spring, and before the other trees have put forth even leaves, it sends forth its beautiful and abundant blossoms. Thus, Jesus has pre-eminence in resurrection, He is the firstborn among many brethren. (Rom. viii. 29.) His victory over death is the sure pledge that the spring-time of youth is at hand for the Church ; even already He calls to His beloved in that beautiful strain of affection, and says, " Rise up, my love, my fair one, and come away. For lo, the winter is past, the rain is over and gone; the flowers appear on the earth; and the time of the singing of birds is come, and the voice of the turtle is heard in our land. The fig-tree putteth forth her green figs, and the vines with the tender grape give a good smell. Arise, my love, my fair one, and come away." (Cant. ii. 10-13.) And as the almond bowls in the central branch point to Him who has "the dew of His youth from the womb of the morning," so also there are similar ornaments in the attendant branches, which point to the Church as itself taking the lead hereafter in resurrection. The same title, " Firstborn," applies to them as well as to the Lord (Heb. xii. 23) ; His early fruitfulness is theirs also ; and they will, in a little while, share in and partake of His spring-time vigour and beauty. Bowls are introduced probably as receptacles for oil, that this vessel might have the fulness of oil dispersed about all parts of it, expressive of the riches of grace held and displayed in Christ and the Church ; for all fulness is in Him, "and of His fulness have all we received, and grace answering to grace." (John L 16.) He is the Christ anointed above His fellows, and to whom God has given the Spirit without measure ; and the Church has received of His anointing ; and so completely is it pervaded by the Spirit, and anointed in Him, its glorious head, that the word " Christ" — the anointed one — is even applied to it as united to Him, as well as being the peculiar name of the Lord Himself. (1 Cor. xii. 12.)

THE KNOPS.

It is difficult to define what kind of ornament the knops were. The word occurs only in two other passages of Scripture, Amos ix. 1 and Zeph. ii. 14, in both of which it is translated "lintel" of a door ; probably some ornament of the cornice over the door. Josephus renders the word "pomegranate;" the Septuagint has <r<j>aLpwTT}p ; and the Vulgate " sphaerula" Besides the four knops connected with the four bowls — "their knops" — there were also three additional knops in the shaft of the Candlestick, a knop being placed under each pair of branches proceeding out of the side. (Exod xxv. 35.) From their situation, thus placed under the branches, I am inclined to think that the knops were like opening buds, from out of which the branches apparently sprouted ; thus expressing more forcibly the fact, that the side branches owed their existence to the fruitfulness of the parent stem. If this were so, the knops would answer to the buds of Aaron's rod, and we shall have the same ornaments in the Candlestick, namely, buds, blossoms, and fruit In the accom- panying drawing, it will be perceived that I have thought it better to retain the round ball of the Septuagint and Vulgate.

THE FLOWERS.

The flowers were the ornaments that especially showed the skill of the workman who fashioned this beautiful vessel, as we learn from Num. viii. 4, where the Candlestick is spoken of as of beaten gold " unto the shaft thereof, and unto the flowers thereof" The Septuagint and Vulgate call them "lilies;" and this is remarkable, as our blessed Lord refers in Matt. vi. 28-30 to this, as being a beautiful flower of the field, when exhorting His disciples to trust in God for the supply of all their need. Solomon, in all his glory, was not arrayed like one of these ; and yet they were but the perishable grass, which to-day is, and to-morrow is cast into the oven. In Isa. xl. 6, and 1 Pet. i. 24, the glory of man is compared to the fleeting beauty of the flower, which withers and falls. In all these passages the flower is an emblem of beauty and glory, though fading and passing away. But these flowers in the Candlestick are of different materials : they are beaten out of solid gold ; they preserve all the beauty and glory, all the exquisite delicacy and loveliness of the flower, but they are of an imperishable substance : their beauty will not fade, their glory will not wither. Thus they are appropriate emblems of the beauty and glory of the new creation. A creation though new, yet founded, as it were, on the ruins of the old ; fashioned of lasting and unfading materials, and yet combining all the beauty and glory of that which shall pass away. The resurrection is the great display of this wisdom and power of God, who is able to fashion anew out of death all that was once fair and glorious, but which has faded and withered ; and to mould and form it afresh in imperishable beauty. The Lord Jesus is the beginning and head of this new creation : He is man in the glory, and the saints, when risen, will still be men ; so that nothing that was glorious or excellent in man, as originally created by God, will be lost, but changed into that which is imperishable and incorruptible. After a heavenly fashion, and of heavenly materials, all will be raised and formed afresh ; and of this He who is now in heaven is the earnest and the pledge. We have borne the image of the earthy ; we can look back at Adam as our head, and see all his goodliness fade like the flower of the grass, yea even his comeliness turned to cor- ruption ; but we shall also bear the image of the heavenly, and the " grace of the fashion thereof" shall not perish, but its beauty will endure, like the imperishable flower of beaten gold.

Pre-eminent in all these emblems of the glory and beauty of new creation stood this Candlestick of gold, with its central shaft and branch; and out of its sides proceeded the six branches, adorned, though in a lesser degree, with like costly ornaments. As a whole, this vessel stood a seven branch Candlestick, characterised by the distinctness and yet unity of its centre and sides; complete in itself, and yet complete because of its appendant branches. The number " seven" is constantly employed in Scripture as emblematical of perfectness as appreciated by God. The work of creation, with its accompanying day of rest, was completed in seven days; and in the Revelation the perfection of power and intelligence is expressed by seven horns and seven eyes, as seen in the Lamb in the midst of the throne. This vessel of the Sanctuary is perfect according to a divine estimate; but its completeness is owing to the six branches that spring from it and are in union with it. So, of Christ and the Church. It derives its life, its fulness from Him; and yet it is His completeness, His fulness — "the fulness of Him that filleth all in all." (Eph. i. 23.) As " the woman is the glory of the man" (1 Cor. xi. 7), and they two are one flesh (Eph. v. 31), so is the Church the glory of Christ, and is one with Him ; so that of believers it can be said, " we are members of His body, of His flesh, and of His bones." (Eph. v. 30.) Christ would be incomplete without the Church, and yet it derives all its completeness, and beauty, and glory from Him; and He and the Church form the one new man, of which Adam and Eve are the type. For " God said, Let us make man in our own image, after our likeness ; and let them have dominion," &c Eve was the completeness of Adam, and yet she was of Adam, distinct from him, and yet the two one flesh. This seems to be shadowed out by the Candlestick standing in the completeness of its beauty, seven branched, and yet distinct as to its centre from the six appended branches ; all forming together a beau- tiful whole, perfect according to the divine estimate of perfection, the number seven.

THE OIL FOR THE LIGHT.

"Oil for the light" is one of the things directed to be brought by the children of Israel, in order that a sanctuary might be made for God to dwell among them. (Exod. xxv. 6.) The rulers of the people brought it, amongst other special and peculiarly costly contributions. (Exod. xxxv. 27, 28.) It was made by the wise-hearted. (Exod. xxxv. 10, 14.) It was to be "pure oil-olive, beaten for the light, to cause the lamp to burn always" (Exod. xxvii. 20); and in Lev. xxiv. 1, 2, the same command is reiterated: " And the Lord spake unto Moses, saying, Command the children of Israel, that they bring unto thee pure oil-olive, beaten for the light, to cause the lamp to burn continually."

The olive-tree is used in Scripture as a type of richness, fertility, and beauty. " But the olive-tree said unto them, Should I leave my fatness, wherewith by me they honour God and man, and go to be promoted over the trees V (Jud. ix. 9.) " But I am like a green olive-tree in the house of God." (Psalm lii. 8.) "The Lord called thy name, A green olive-tree, fair, and of goodly fruit" (Jer. xi. 16.) " His branches shall spread, and his beauty shall be as the olive-tree, and his smell as Lebanon." (Hos. xiv. 6.) The oil was to be beaten, not squeezed from the olive, that it might be more clear and pure; the spontaneous outflowing from the fruit, rather than forced out by pressure. Oil-olive is thus a beautiful emblem of the rich and ever fresh presence and grace of the Spirit. The Candlestick with its golden lamps, causing light "to ascend" continually in the Sanctuary, through the pure oil- olive constantly supplied, is an expressive type of the Church in union with Christ, bearing up the fulness of light and glory in the presence of God, anointed and fed by the fulness of the blessed Spirit, which has been given without measure unto Him. "Grace has been poured into his lips," and " of his fulness have all we received, and grace for grace;" in the glory of God will all that rich and unspeakable grace be displayed. There the fresh graces of the Spirit will shine forth unhindered ; life and light will there be manifested in perfect and everlasting excellency ; and the riches of the glory of God's inheritance in the saints will be displayed in all their eternal value and fulness.

This holy vessel has the epithet "pure" attached to it. (Exod. xxxi. 8 ; xxxix. 37; and Lev. xxiv. 4.) How chaste and pure must every thing be that stands in the light of the glory of God; and especially how clear and spotless must that be, which has to bear up the light in His presence. This Candlestick shed not its light on earth; it stood in the holy place, one of those places made with hands which prefigured the true heavenly courts. It represents Christ and the Church, not as the light of this world below, but as presented before God in the heavens above, sustaining light even there, and sending forth its radiance in the midst of that light which no man can approach unto. Soon Christ will raise the Church in unfading glory, and " present it to Himself a glorious Church, not having spot or wrinkle, or any such thing. " (Eph. v. 27.) In a little while He will "present us faultless before the presence of His glory with exceeding joy" (Jude 24); pure like the golden Candlestick, fit to stand in the light of the glory, and to be the depository of light in the presence of God.

THE PURPOSE OF THE LIGHT.

The light sent forth by this beautiful vessel, though proceeding from seven lamps, yet was but one light; the lamps are never said to send forth their lights, but light ; the oil ministered to each was the same, and is always specified as oil for the light, not for the lamps. Again, in Exod. xxvii. 20, and Lev. xxiv. 2, it will be found that the expression is used, "to cause the lamp to burn always," not the lamps. (Our translation is wrong in Lev. xxiv. 2, where it ought to be " the lamp," as may be seen by reference to the Hebrew.) This use of the word "light" and also " lamp, leads our thoughts to the blessed unity of the light, though proceeding from seven distinct lamps; and the unity of the lamps themselves, which, though seven, yet formed but one. And will it not be so in the glory hereafter? Will not each member of Christ, though distinct in himself, and shining with his own indi- vidual glory, yet be one with Christ and the Church ; so that the light of each will be the light of all, and one bright irradiation of glory will shine forth from the whole? The Church and Christ will be but the one lamp, though there will be pre-eminence in Him, and distinctness in them; and it will send forth but one light, though proceeding from various sources.

There are three purposes specified for which this golden vessel with its seven lamps of light stood in the Sanctuary of God. The first was that it might shed its light " before the Lord." " And he lighted the lamps before the Lord, as the Lord commanded Moses." (Exod. xl. 25; see also Exod xxvii. 21 and Lev. xxiv. 4.) The Candlestick shed its light in God's presence : He could look upon its perfectness and beauty; even He "who is light, and in Him is no darkness at all," could delight in the brightness of these seven lamps of light, and His Sanctuary was enlivened by them. What a holy and glorious standing has the Church of God — to find its place, its home, in the presence of God, to be under His eye, and dwell in the light of His glory; and not only so, but to have the glory "revealed in us" (Rom viii. 18); and to have that glory given to us which has been given to Christ " And the glory which thou gavest me I have given them ; that they may be one, even as we are one : I in them, and thou in me, that they may be made perfect in one." (John xvii. 22.)

A second purpose of the light we gather from Exod. xxvi. 35: "And thou shalt set the table without the vail, and the Candlestick over against the table on the side of the Tabernacle, towards the south; and thou shalt put the table on the north side:" and Exod. xl. 24, " And he put the Candlestick in the Tabernacle of the Congregation, over against the table, on the side of the Tabernacle southward." Thus, it was placed opposite to, and cast its light upon, the Shewbread Table; thereby displaying the whiteness and purity of the twelve loaves, covered with frankincense arranged on it. So the display of the Church in glory around the Lord will shed back light again upon the past, and will bring out into bright and blessed manifestation the value of Him who has been here down into death for it: the perfectness of His obedience, and the costliness of His sacrifice, will be plainly told out by the glory with which the Church will be crowned.

The third and chief object of the light is expressed in Exod. xxv. 37 : " And thou shalt make the seven lamps thereof, and they shall light the lamps thereof, that they may give light over against it;" and Num. viii. 2, 3, "Speak unto Aaron, and say unto him, when thou lightest the lamps, the seven lamps shall give light over against the Candlestick. And Aaron did so; he lighted the lamps thereof over against the Candlestick, as the Lord commanded Moses." The difficult phrase " over against it," found in Exod. xxv., is thus explained to mean, "over against the Candlestick." One chief object of the light was to illumine, and thereby display, the Candlestick itself; for "this work of the Candlestick was of beaten gold, unto the shaft thereof, unto the flowers thereof, beaten work."

All the light and glory of the Church to be manifested hereafter in blessed union with the Lord will only the more exhibit the love, wisdom, and power of God, as seen in raising Christ from the dead, and giving Him to be head over all things to it. In the fulness of His own light, and of that of the Church, Christ will be manifested, " glorified in his saints." The more their light and glory shine forth, the more will His beauty and perfectness be seen, and the more will the wisdom and s'dlfulness of God be displayed. The seven lamps alike lighted up, and made manifest the solid shaft of beaten gold, and the lovely and delicate flowers of the branch. The might and excellency of strength, as well as the beauty and glory of the Lord, will be fully declared in and by the Church in resurrection ; it will shine forth to accomplish one great counsel of God, namely, " that we shall be to the praise of His glory."

TIME OF LIGHTING AND DRESSING THE LAMPS.

And Aaron shall burn thereon (on the incense altar) sweet incense every morning ; when he dresseth the lamps, he shall burn incense upon it. And when Aaron light eth the lamps at even, he shall burn incense upon it. (Exod. xxx. 7, 8.) Aaron and his sons shall order it from evening to morning before the Lord. (Exod. xxvii. 21.) Aaron shall order it from the evening unto the morning before the Lord continually. (Lev. xxiv. 3.)

When the princes of this world had crucified the Lord of glory, and had thereby quenched the " true light," and the darkness of night began imperceptibly to steal over the world, a light sprang up in the presence of God, with its perfect sevenfold lustre, transferred from the earth, and shedding for the first time, its radiance in the sanctuary above. Christ was received up in the glory of resurrection, just at the time when men thought they had made all sure for retaining Him in the place of death; " sealing the stone and setting a watch." The grave is the last place where the world has beheld Christ; a risen Christ is unknown to it and is its certain condemnation. Light and life banished from hence, but centred in and around the Lord, have found their eternal resting-place above : and the Church of God, in like manner as its risen head, unknown and despised by a world of darkness, stands in union with Him in glory, and finds its life and its light there. There is a passage in John xiii. 30-32 which expresses some of these truths. Satan, the prince of this world, had obtained full power over Judas, and that by means of the world's great object of desire and attraction — the mammon of unrighteousness ; and all was now ready for the accomplishment of his fearful deed of sin, the betrayal of the Lord : he went out to that end, and the Scripture emphatically adds, " it was night" The glorious light was about to be quenched ; the night had set in. Those lips which had spoken life and truth were about to be closed in the silence of death, and the doom of this world was fixed : henceforth there was to be a night of sin, and darkness, and death ; henceforth the world was to be under " rulers of darkness," till He whom it had rejected and slain should return as "the Sun of righteousness with healing in His wings." But the Son of man would be glorified on earth, even in His obedience unto death, and God would be glorified in Him. The cross, the place of shame and death, would be the true glory of the Son of man ; and God Himself would be glorified in that blessed and crowning act of His Son's obedience ; and if so, God would raise Him from the dead, and glorify Him in Himself, yea "would straightway glorify Him."

The heavens were opened to receive the rejected and despised One; the heavenly tabernacle above became the place of His joy and glory.

Even so light was presented to God in His sanctua^yust as the darkness of night set in ; when the evening cast its gloomy shadows over the world, the " Lamp of God" was lighted, and sent forth its brilliant rays in the holy place, This holy vessel, thus lighted in the evening, was dressed in the morning. This points onward to a period still future, when the night shall have passed, and the day shall dawn The first ushering in of that blessed day will be the raising and presenting the Church to God in the full effulgence of light and glory. During the whole of the night, indeed, light is in the sanctuary, for Christ is there, like the seven-branch candlestick of gold; and faith already sees the Church there also, united to Him, and complete in Him. But the night is even now far spent, and the day is at hand, the resurrection day, the morning without clouds ; and then the Church will in reality be raised and presented in glory and beauty, and the glory and beauty of Christ will be complete. The day began, according to the scriptural method of reckoning, with the preceding evening; "the evening and the morning were the first day;" so throughout Gen. i. In one sense the day has already begun, for Christ has risen, and the evening that precedes the morning has commenced. The lamp has already been lighted; even now it sheds its perfect light in the heavenly tabernacle; but the High Priest will, ere long, cause it to burn with increased brilliancy. He will dress the lamps; He will, by the power of the Spirit, cause the Church to shine in bright and undimmed glory forever. The resurrection day is not the commencement of the glory of the Church, for already it is united to, and glorified in a risen Christ ; but it is the completion of its glory, and it is the time of its full display in perfection of light and beauty before the Lord.

The constant repetition of lighting and dressing the lamps may present a difficulty to some ; but it will be found with this, as well as with many other typical actions, that the fact of repetition only proves the insufficiency of the Levitical order to accomplish anything. The priests themselves succeeded one another, because "they could not continue by reason of death;" their priestly power availed nothing. Death, the very foe over whom they should, as priests, have triumphed, became their conqueror. The sacrifices were daily and yearly repeated; for the blood shed therein affected nothing. In fact, " the law made nothing perfect," and was a mere shadow of good things to come. In contrast to all this, we have a priest that " abideth xontinually;" one who can " save to the very end;" a sacrifice that needeth not to be repeated; for the shedding of that blood has accomplished forever the remission of sins; a candlestick in the sanctuary that needs not to be re-lighted, for it ceases not to shed its lustre before the Lord. The Scriptures of the New Testament, also, abundantly supply passages which prove that the period of Christ's absence is one uninterrupted night; and that the return of Christ, and the resurrection of the saints, is the morning of a bright and endless day of glory.

There are two or three other things that may be noticed respecting this beautiful vessel One is, that there is no foot or pedestal described on which it stood or rested ; another is, that there are no dimensions given as to its height or breadth. Our thoughts are hereby led to the unearthly standing of the Church; it has no home, no resting-place below; its rest, its place is in the heavens; it has no foot, no dependence on or connection with earth. Moreover, no measurements are given; for the Church can be defined by no earthly standard. Its length and breadth and height of glory cannot be estimated by human thought or calculation. The Spirit of God alone can reveal those "deep things of God. He alone can instruct the soul in that glory which " eye hath not seen, nor ear heard, and which it hath not entered into the heart of man to conceive." " The measure of the stature of the fulness of Christ" can alone be estimated by "the breadth and length and depth and height of the love of Christ, which passeth knowledge." A third remarkable fact connected with the ordering of the vessel is, that in the directions given for lighting and dress- ing the lamps, in Exod. xxx. 7, 8, Lev. xxiv. 3, and Num. viii. 1-3, Aaron is alone mentioned as the one who is to undertake that service. It was peculiarly a work entrusted to the high priest, and to him only. We easily see the immediate typical reference here to the Lord Jesus Himself as our great High Priest, to whose Rvmg power and love God has alone entrusted the glory and safe keeping of the Church, and who only is able to present it 4< a glorious Church, without spot or wrinkle, or any such thing."

It is one chief source of rest and joy to our souls to know, that Christ has kept, and will still preserve, His saints in undimmed light and glory, presented to God above. However, the Church has been scattered and broken — however its light has become obscured, or well-nigh quenched here on earth, yet above it has been, and still is, sustained in unfailing lustre, united to its glorious head. The eye of faith has but to turn away from gazing at the defilements, corruptions, and darkness of this world, and to look into the sanctuary of God, and there it will behold one who, like the solid shaft, steadily and unweariedly bears up light before the Lord, on behalf of the saints; and who, like the branch also, with its lovely flowers and fruit, presents unfading beauty and glory in His presence. The morning of the Lord's return will prove how Christ has maintained His position before God on behalf of the Church, notwithstanding all its declension and failure ; and how, in consequence, He is able to present it "faultless before the presence of His glory with exceeding joy."

THE VESSELS ATTACHED TO THE CANDLESTICK.

Exod. xxv. 38-40. — And the tongs thereof, Exod. xxxvii. 23, 24. — And he made his and the snuff- dishes thereof, shall be of pure seven lamps, and his snuffers, and his snuff- gold. Of a talent of pure gold shall he make it, dishes, of pure gold. Of a talent of pure gold with aU these vessels. And look that thou make made he it, and aU the vessels thereof, them after their pattern, which had shewed thee in the mount.

THE TONGS.

The ward E^nj^D, translated in Exod. xxxvii. 23 "snuffers," is rendered "tongs" in all other places where it occurs; and this seems to be the correct translation. It is only found elsewhere in Num. iv. 9, 1 Kings vii. 49, 2 Chron. iv. 21, and Isa. vi. 6. The use of these instruments would be twofold. On the one hand they would be needed at the Candlestick, when the priest dressed the lamps, to raise up the wick, in order that the light might burn more brightly ; besides this, it would seem that they were needed at the incense altar for placing the live coals on it, or removing them into the censer when that vessel was used. The dressing the lamps in the morning has been adverted to above, as affording a type of the resurrection of the Church. This ministry and power of Christ, which will present the Church to God complete in light and glory, are foreshadowed in the use and appointment of these golden tongs. The high priest by means of them would cause the lamp to shine with its daylight splendour in the Tabernacle, just as the morning was breaking on the mountains of the world outside. As the Sanctuary had a light of its own, shedding forth its radiance within, whilst the world was in the darkness of night ; so also it had its own peculiar light during the day, when the night of the world was over, and the glorious sun began to arise. The act of raising the wick, and thus causing the lamp to burn in full brilliancy, would answer to that beautiful expression of the apostle (2 Cor. v. 4), "that mortality might be swallowed up of life." It would not be re-lighting an extinguished lamp, nor cutting off a smouldering wick ; but gently raising the wick, so that what was before dim might disappear in the brightness of its increased light So one of the chief glories of the resurrection day is the sudden CHANGE of that which is now weak and worthless, into glory and beauty. " Who shall change our vile body, that it may be fashioned like unto His glorious body, according to the working whereby He is able even to subdue all things unto Himself." (Phil. hi. 21.) When the night had closed in, and was well-nigh spent, the priest that was watching in the holy place would be reminded, as his eye glanced at the golden tongs by the side of the Candlestick, that the morning would soon dawn, when light in all its fulness would be shed forth before the Lord from that seven-branch luminary ; and when also to the world itself the sun would arise with genial warmth and splendour.

The tongs seem also for special use at the incense altar. There were no other instruments provided in the Sanctuary for handling the live coals; and from Isa. vi. 6, we find that tongs were used by one of the seraphim in the temple, and the burning coal was taken in them from off the altar. The reason for keeping instruments of this kind by the Candlestick, when they were used in ministration at the incense altar, has been adverted to under the Vessels of the Shewbread Table, and is enlarged upon under the following head.

THE SNUFF-DISHES OR CENSERS

The Hebrew word HFlTO is translated "snuff-dish" in connection with the Candlestick only, and that in Exod. xxv. 38, xxxvii. 23, and Num. iv. 9 : in every other place (and it occurs often) it is translated "censer" or "firepan" The expression " snuff-dish," in these places connected with the Candlestick, may have arisen from a difficulty in the mind of the translator to understand the use of a censer to a Candlestick; and therefore he converted the "censer" into a "snuff-dish," and the "tongs" into "snuffers," as apparently more in unison with the vessel with which they were connected. But in dressing a lamp, neither would snuffers nor snuff- dishes be needed. The universal use of these vessels in all other places in Scripture for censers, would of itself induce one to suppose that here also they must mean the same. There were also vessels of the same name, made of brass, and connected with the altar of burnt-offering, called in Exod. xxvii. 3 and xxxviii. 3 " firepans,"' and Num. iv. 14 "censers."

The ancient censer was merely a pan of gold or brass to receive the burning coals, with a long handle attached to it, wherewith the priest was able to carry it full of fire. On the burning coals thus carried, incense was thrown. The reason for connecting golden censers with the Candlestick, and not with the incense altar, was to link together and combine the different vessels of ministry in all the great acts of priestly service. For example, on the great day of atonement, the High Priest would take the golden censer from the Candlestick, fill it with burning coals from the altar of incense, take his hands full of incense from the Shewbread Table, and then cast the incense on the fire in the censer before the Ark, in the most holy place. In this one great act of priestly service, all the vessels of the Sanctuary would be involved : the altar, with its holy fire, would yield the live coals ; the Candlestick would yield the censer ; the Shewbread Table, with its golden spoons, would yield the incense; and all would have reference to making atonement before the Ark and Mercy Seat. The high priest would bear in his thoughts the varied excellences and purposes of the different vessels of the Sanctuary, whilst he sprinkled the blood, the foundation on which all priestly ministry was conducted. The varied service at those vessels was a result from, and dependent on, the great work of atone- ment. Moreover, the censers at the Candlestick, which were to bear the holy fire, betokened the intimate union between LIGHT and HOLINESS; besides forming a link between the vessel of light and the incense altar, the place from whence sweet perfume ascended to God.

How this directs our souls to the one glorious chain of priestly service, con- ducted by our blessed Lord on behalf of His saints : each portion is but a link of one continuous whole ; the atonement is the basis on which it all rests, and from which it all springs; the end is the presentation of the saints, perfect and complete, in the day of glory.

It may be remarked, in conclusion, that the Candlestick and its attendant vessels, to a certain extent, formed by themselves a complete whole, being made out of a definite mass of gold appropriated to that special purpose: "of a talent of pure gold shall he make it, with all these vessels." The injunction, also, " Look that thou make them after their pattern, which was shewed thee in the mount," is twice repeated, as immediately connected with the Candlestick, in Exod. xxv. 40 and Num. viii. 4. All this adds value and importance to this holy vessel, and proves it to be one preeminently precious in the sight of the Lord, and that it has a peculiar aspect and standing, and a glory of its own, distinct from the earth, and connected immediately with the heavens.

We have but little recorded in the Word respecting the Candlestick subsequent to its being formed and placed in the Tabernacle. There are, however, two remarkable and contrasted scenes of judgment, in which an allusion is made to it; the. one in 1 Sam. iii., the other in Dan. v. In the early days of Samuel the priesthood of Israel had grievously departed from the Lord. The ways of the sons of Eli were in fearful opposition to the holiness and truth of God; and their father was content with merely rebuking their evil and allowed his faithfulness to yield to his natural affection. But the Candle- stick still burned in the Sanctuary. There was yet a standard of light and truth, against which the priests had sinned, and by which they would be judged. " The lamp of God," with its sevenfold lustre, stood in solemn and fearful contrast with their ways of darkness and sin; and, "ere it went out," the word came to Samuel of sweeping wrath and judgment on the whole house of Eli, so that " the ears of every one that heard it should tingle." Here the lamp of God was the witness that "judgment must begin at the house of God;" the priests of the Lord had not walked according to the light of the Sanctuary, but had followed a path of unholiness and evil; their ways especially called for judgment, when viewed in contrast with the purity and light of that heavenly vessel, which stood as the pattern of what the calling and character of those should be who ministered before the Lord. May we not gather important instruction from this history? As priests to God, consecrated by the blood of Christ, and the anointing of the Holy Spirit, believers have a heavenly standard of perfectness and glory, in the light of which they have to walk, and to fashion their ways, and to form their estimates of things around them. The light of the glory is the judgment of the flesh and its lusts — of the world and its ways. "If ye then be risen with Christ," says the Apostle, " seek those things which are above, where Christ sitteth on the right hand of God: set your affection on things above, not on things on the earth." (Col. iii. 1, 2.) And again, "For ye were sometimes darkness, but now are ye light in the Lord: walk as children of light and have no fellowship with the unfruitful works of darkness, but rather reprove them." (Eph. v. 8, 11.)

In one other scene of judgment, but of a different character, this holy vessel is again found. (Dan. v.) Belshazzar the king made a great feast and displayed his earthly power and magnificence to a thousand of his lords. Not content with this, he ordered the holy vessels of the Temple to be brought to adorn his triumph and gratify his pride. Their presence sealed the doom of the king. " In the same hour came forth fingers of a man's hand and wrote ova' against the candlestick^ upon the plaster of the wall of the king's palace: MENE, MENE, TEKEL, UPHARSIN." Have we not here portents of a coming judgment? Does not this last act of Belshazzar's iniquity, in desecrating the holy vessels of the Temple, depict some of the closing features of the world's sin? The king had sought to lower the God of heaven to the level of " the gods of gold and of silver, of brass, of iron, of wood, and of stone." He had praised the senseless idols of his own creating, instead of glorifying the God " in whose hand was his breath, and all his ways." In seeking to advance his own glory, he unconsciously introduced into the scene his own judg- ment The holy vessels, those types of heavenly glory and perfectness, were standards against which God would weigh this monarch of the earth. The Candlestick of gold, with its completeness of light and beauty, stood in bright but solemn contrast with the vanity and blasphemy around. The finger of the man's hand, that same hour, inscribed on the wall the sentence, " Thou art weighed in the balances, and art found wanting." Here are traces of evil and of judgment which will have their full accom- plishment in these latter days. Man, in his pride and folly will exalt himself, and his own acts and ways, above the God of heaven. He will praise his gods — his own wisdom, power, and skill. He will desecrate the name of God and of Christ; even at this hour he only ranks those holy names on a level with the gods of the world. But the Most High will bring all this pride and blasphemy into contrast with the true glory of Christ and the Church. The hand of a man will again write the sentence of judgment: " For God has appointed a day, in the which He will judge the world in righteousness, by that MAN whom He hath ordained." (Acts xvii. 31.) Christ, once despised and rejected, "will come with ten thousand of His saints to execute judgment upon all, and to convince all that are ungodly among them of all their ungodly deeds, which they have ungodly committed ; and of all their hard speeches, which ungodly sinners have spoken against Him." (Jude 15.) Even now the believer sees by the eye of faith the sentence written on the plastered palaces of the earth, " God hath numbered thy kingdom, and finished it." When the mystery of iniquity has reached its climax, and the man of sin shall have exalted himself " above all that is called God, or that is worshipped," then will come the sudden and over- whelming judgment, and destruction of the power and greatness of this world. Christ and the risen Church will be the standard against which all the vanity and passing splendour of earth will be weighed. The Candlestick of Gold is a sure witness of the approaching joy and exaltation of the Church, and of the certain judgment and overturning of the nations. "The kingdoms of this world are become the kingdoms of our Lord and of His Christ, and He shall reign for ever and ever." (Rev xi. 15,)

1 From I Chron. xxviii. 15 and 1 Kings vii. 49, we learn that there were ten Candlesticks of gold made for the Temple, according to patterns given by the Spirit to David, and described by him to Solomon. There were also Candlesticks of silver. And in Jer. lii. 19, the Candlesticks are mentioned amongst other vessels taken to Babylon. But from 2 Chron. xiii. 1 1 and Dan. v. 5, it would seem, that there was one Candlestick especially distinguished; and this may have been the original Candlestick of the Tabernacle.

In the drawing of the Candlestick, vessels have been arranged around it so as to conceal any foot, since none is mentioned in Scripture ; also there are golden vessels represented which are not mentioned in Exodus, but which are enumerated in Num. iv. 9; "all the oil vessels thereof these have been inserted in the drawing, in order more effectually to hide the foot. 1 * It will be perceived that the drawing of the Candlestick, accompanying this letter-press, has been designed according to the description thus afforded by the text, and materially differs from the representation of the

Candlestick on the arch of Titus, in this respect especially, that the central branch is much higher than the side branches. The design on the arch is clearly incorrect, as regards the pedestal on which the vessel rests ; for it is there pictured as adorned with sea monsters : this proves that either the Jews had fashioned a new candlestick for the Temple after their return from captivity, and had not regarded the language of Scripture as to its description ; or that the Roman artist pleased his own taste when he represented the vessels borne in triumph, and varied them so as to suit his own ideas of beauty. At all events we cannot depend on these sculptures as being truthful representations of the vessels. It does not appear that the original Candlestick was restored to the Temple after the return, as it is not enumerated amongst the vessels in Ezra i. 9-1 1. If anyone is desirous of a correct representation of the Candlestick, as sculptured on the arch of Titus, such will be found in Reland's little work, **De Spoliis Templi," the plates of which are interesting, because taken from drawings on the spot many years ago, before the bas-reliefs were so defaced as they have since been, by the Jews constantly endeavouring to erase them.

THE ALTAR OF THE INCENSE

Exod. xxx. 1-5. — And thou shalt make an altar to burn incense upon; of shittim-wood shalt thou make it. A cubit shall be the length thereof, and a cubit the breadth thereof; foursquare shall it be; and two cubits shall be the height thereof: the horns thereof shall be of the same. And thou shalt overlay it with pure gold, the top thereof, and the sides thereof round about, and the horns thereof : and thou shalt make unto it a crown of gold round about And two golden rings shalt thou make to it under the crown of it, by the two corners thereof, upon the two sides of it shalt thou make it ; and they shall be for places for the staves to bear it withal. And thou shalt make the staves of shittim-wood and overlay them with gold.

Exod. xxxvii. 25-28. — And he made the in- cense altar of shittim-wood : the length of it was a cubit, and the breadth of it a cubit ; it was foursquare ; and two cubits was the height of it ; the horns thereof were of the same. And he over- laid it with pure gold, both the top of it, and the sides thereof round about, and the horns of it: also, he made unto it a crown of gold round about. And he made two rings of gold for it under the crown thereof, by the two corners of it, upon the two sides thereof, to be places for the staves to bear it withal. And he made the staves of shittim-wood and overlaid them with gold.

THERE were two Altars attached to the Tabernacle — one the Brazen Altar, called also the Altar of burnt-offering, which stood in the court, — the other, the Golden Altar, or Altar of sweet incense, which stood in the holy place. All Israel had access to the former; but the priests alone could approach the latter. On the one death was perpetually recorded, and blood was sprinkled and poured out; on the other no sacrificial victims were to be offered, but the fragrance of sweet spices was constantly to ascend from thence to God. Truths connected with atone- ment for sin ; cleansing from defilement by means of blood, and acceptance through the death of the victim, were more immediately taught by the ministrations at the brazen altar; whilst the high calling and standing of the saint, the preserving him in that standing, so as to offer acceptable worship in the heavenlies, and maintenance of communion and intercourse with God, are subjects more directly connected with the altar of gold. Yet both are intimately and inseparably linked together. The Incense Altar owed its standing to the blood of atonement (Exod. xxx. 10) : it was an altar and therefore had reference to, and was the result of, a sacrifice already presented ; and the holy fire which caused the sweet perfume to ascend, was that which had first descended and consumed the victim on the altar of burnt-offering.

It is to be observed that the Incense Altar is not described in due order with the other vessels of the Tabernacle. The 25th chapter of Exodus, as we have seen, describes the Ark, Table, and Candlestick ; the subject then suddenly changes, and instead of getting, as we might have expected, the account of this altar, the 26th chapter opens with various details respecting the construction of the Tabernacle ; then follow descriptions of the brazen altar, and the court of the Tabernacle, suc- ceeded by two chapters containing directions for making the garments of glory and beauty, and for the consecration of the priesthood ; and the 30th chapter reverts to the interior of the holy place, and opens with the description of the Altar of Incense. Especial importance is thus given, and peculiar interest attaches to this golden vessel. It was one which betokened the highest priestly ministration: its place was within the Tabernacle: it represented therefore a ministry in heaven itself. From its summit a cloud of fragrance constantly rolled upwards before the Lord, typifying an active ministry in His presence. The Tabernacle is first described, wherein this fragrance was to be developed; the brazen altar is also previously appointed, because this priestly service was a result of the value and efficacy of the sacrifice ; and the garments, and consecration of the high priest and his sons are detailed, in order that the glory, beauty, and lofty standing of those who were to serve at this altar might be set forth, before the vessel itself is described.

THE MATERIALS OF THE ALTAR

We again observe the same materials, wood and gold, employed in the construction of this holy vessel. Their typical import has been alluded to before. The first and second chapters of the Hebrews have a connection with the subsequent details in that epistle, respecting the sacrifice and priesthood of the Lord, very similar to that which exists between the materials of the holy vessels, and the various uses for which they were fashioned. In that blessed portion of the Word of God, the Spirit describes the nature and glories of Him who is both the Lamb of God and the Great High Priest;— THE SON, in all the dignity of His nature as God, and also as man ; who came here to suffer, and was raised from the dead, a priest for ever after the order of Melchisedec. All the value and efficacy of the sacrifice, and all the power and glory of the priesthood, depend on the wondrous truths therein detailed respecting HIS person. The kingly and priestly offices He holds do not, like mere human honours, ennoble Him; but gain their excellency and value from the nature and being of Him who sustains them. In human arrangements the person is ennobled by the titles conferred: but God tells us of THE SON; and His intrinsic dignity, power, and glory render precious and efficient every office He bears. To estimate aright the value of the sacrifice, we must know the person of the Lamb Himself ; to rest happily on the power of the priest, we must be instructed as to HIM who is the priest As then the materials of the Incense Altar, and other vessels of the Sanctuary, are first enumerated, and their uses subsequently detailed ; so our souls are first directed to the nature and person of the Lord Jesus, and after- wards His sacrifice and priesthood are blessedly set forth.

THE DIMENSIONS OF THE ALTAR.

All the altars described in Scripture were "foursquare? their length and breadth being equal (Exod. xxxviii. i; Ezek. xliii. 16.) A square is a compact, even-sided figure; and seems to have been especially selected for the form of the altars, in order to represent the completeness and fulness of the work effected thereon, whether of sacrifice or incense. The same perfect measure and estimate was thus presented every way, whether towards God, or towards man. Firmness also, and stability, are betokened by the square figure.

This altar stood above the other measured vessels of the Sanctuary; the Ark and Table of Shewbread being only a cubit and a half high, whereas the height of this vessel was two cubits. Thus it took the lead in the Tabernacle ; its summit rose more to a level with the dwelling-place of God, " between the Cherubim, over the mercy-seat;" and thence was wafted the fragrant cloud, which sheltered under its perfume both the priest who ministered, and the other vessels of the Sanctuary. This teaches us the lofty standing of our great High Priest in the glory of God. His first entrance there from the earth — a man in resurrection — added a new and sweet odour to the dwelling-place of God. A cloud of human fragrance rolled up and could mingle itself with the cloud of divine glory, and the heavenly Tabernacle was filled with the holy perfume. The intercession of Him who " is pure and holy," still meets the light and glory of God's presence in our behalf. It covers over every ill-savour that otherwise might be wafted from the worshipper on earth into the holy place ; it presents fragrance immediately " before the Lord," so that no weakness, no failing on the part of His people, may hinder their ready access to the throne of grace. What must the heavenly calling of the saints be, when such a High Priest was not only needed, but " became us, who is holy, harmless, undefiled, separate from sinners, and made higher than the heavens. " (Heb. vii. 26.)

THE HORNS OF THE ALTAR.

Horns are peculiarly a characteristic of all the altars of which a description is given in the Word of God. (See Exod. xxvii. 2 ; xxx. 2; Ezek. xliii. 15.) The readers of Scripture are familiar with the constant use of these emblems, as types of power and dignity. We need only refer to the Psalms and the book of Daniel, for a multitude of passages where they are thus employed. The power and strength of the altars seem to have been concentrated in the horns. As the most prominent parts, the eye would naturally first be attracted to them ; the command so constantly to place the blood there, showed that God also had especial regard to these distinctive portions of the holy vessels ; and the hand of him who desired to claim the power and protection of the altar laid hold of them. To " bind the sacrifice with cords, even unto the horns of the altar," is one use of the horns of the brazen altar mentioned in the 118th Psalm, ver. 27. The scene there depicted is one of joy and thanksgiving ; and the blessing of God's light and deliverance has been so fully realized, that the exhortation is to bring up the peace or thanksgiving sacrifice, and be ready to slay it at once, close to the altar; so that no interval may elapse between the consciousness of God's mercy received, and the return of praise and thanksgiving to Him. To bind the peace-sacrifice even to the horns of the altar, is thus a beautiful way of expressing the soul's desire, immediately to celebrate God's mercy ; and that in the only way in which it can be truly estimated, namely, through the death of the Lamb ; tracing up every deliverance, every blessing at once to its true source — the love of God in having given His only-begotten Son to die.

In the drawings of the Incense Altar it will be perceived that it stands corner- wise; having an angle, and consequently a horn, turned towards the spectator, instead of a side. This position has been adopted from a consideration of the text, with reference especially to the staves. It will be seen from Exod. xxx. 4, and xxxvii. 27, that there were only two rings for the staves, instead of four; and that these rings were placed at two corners, immediately under the crown. This would necessitate the vessel being carried corner-%vise y instead of what we should familiarly term square; and as it was carried, so it would be deposited, and stand in the Tabernacle. The object of this variation from all the other vessels of the Taber- nacle which had staves (each of the others having four rings), was, it is believed, in order to direct a horn of the Altar towards each part of Israel's host The Tabernacle itself stood east and west ; and the four camps of Israel took up their several positions with reference to this holy dwelling ; Judah, east ; Reuben, south ; Ephraim, west ; and Dan, north. If the Altar were turned angularly in the holy place, a horn would then point towards each of these four camps, and the incense from its summit would have equal reference, in all its value and power, to each portion of the hosts of the Lord. Does not this afford us a true type of the intercession of Christ, offered alike in all its value and fragrance for every portion of His people? — the savour of that sweet perfume ascending with reference to the north, south, east, and west ; and its efficacy and fulness alike presented on behalf of every believer. Now that the people of God are scattered, as it were, to the four winds of heaven, separated one from another, and broken up in little fragments, how comforting is it to remember that all are presented by Christ in unbroken unity, and in full perfectness before God ! All are sheltered under the one fragrant cloud of incense; all are alike accepted in the Beloved; and He who is " pure and holy," ever liveth to make intercession on behalf of all.

THE CROWN AND STAVES.

The Incense Altar, like the Ark and Table of Shewbread, had its " crown of gold round about" It has been stated before, that the " crown " was a ledge extending above the top of the vessel it encircled, to retain fixedly in their proper positions the Mercy Seat covering the Ark, and the Shewbread arranged on the table. The object of the similar rim of gold around the top of this altar, was to prevent the coals of fire, or the holy perfume, being displaced or scattered. It will be observed that the two golden rings for the staves are directed to be placed "under the crown:" this intimates that there was some connection between the crown and the staves which bare the vessel on the journey. There is no provision made in Num. iv., where the directions respecting the march occur, for moving the coals or incense off the golden Altar when it was carried. The fire and perfume were supposed to remain burning on it, even during the march: the golden crown would therefore hold an important office, preventing any displacement of these holy things, when the Altar was borne on the shoulders of the Levites. The more Israel trembled, or tottered, on the rugged path through the wilderness, the greater the need of this ceaseless perfume. Their murmurings would be called forth by the difficulties or privations of the way; the flesh would exhibit many a varied phase of corruption; the faint heart of unbelief would cause the knees to become feeble, and to fail. The saints of God, like Israel of old, have dangers, difficulties, and temptations besetting them on their road; and many a weakness, corruption, and failing is manifested. How needful that the continuance of uninterrupted intercession should be secured ; that a sweet savour of Christ should take the place of murmurings and short-comings ; that a cloud of incense should travel onward with the hosts of the Lord, till they are presented faultless in the presence of His glory ! Is it not blessed to see, in the golden circle crowning this Altar, a sure provision for the maintenance of " purity and holiness," even in the presence of God, on behalf of His weak and erring people? We may write three gracious sentences of truth on the three several crowns that surround respectively the golden vessels of the Tabernacle. On the crown around the Ark, "His mercy endureth FOR EVER :" on that which retains the Shewbread ever in its right position on the table, under the eye of God, " NOW in the presence of God for us: n and on that around the Incense Altar, "He EVER Ivveth to make intercession for us"

THE PLACE OF THE ALTAR.

As we have before observed, the situation of the Incense Altar was in the holy place. It had also direct reference, as to its position in the Sanctuary, to the Ark and Mercy Seat. " And thou shalt put it before the vail that is by the ark of the testimony, before the mercy seat that is over the testimony, where I will meet with thee." (Exod.

xxx. 6.) " And thou shalt set the Altar of gold for the Incense before the Ark of the testimony." (Exod xl. 5.) This command Moses fulfilled, as related (Exod. xl 26), by placing the "golden Altar in the tent of the congregation before the vail" From these passages it appears plain that this vessel was set in the holy place, so as to be directly opposite the Ark; and though the vail intervened, separating the holy place from the most holy, yet this Altar was considered to be immediately "before the mercy seat." One of the names also characterizing it and distinguishing it from the Altar of Burnt-offering, is the Altar " before the Lord.' 1 (Lev. iv. 7, 18; xvL 18.) In Rev. viii. 3, it is designated as "the golden Altar which was before the throne." As to its position, it had direct reference to God's presence " between the cherubim, over the mercy seat," standing in the path which led into the holiest, where His glory was manifested ; and anyone who would approach thither, so as to enter the very dwelling-place of God, must pass this Altar in the way. 1 We are hereby reminded of our need of the sweet fragrance of the name of Jesus, and the value and power of His intercession, in order that we come into the presence of God with confidence, and present acceptable worship to Him. Our watchful High Priest, like the golden Altar in the way, stands ever ready to add fragrance to our petitions, and render sweet our service. He bade His disciples ask in His Name, that they might receive, and that their joy might be full (John xvi. 24.) We speak in His name to God : all its preciousness attaches to our prayers ; and that because He, the living witness of purity and holiness, is ever before the Lord for us ; Himself a speaking testimony and proof of the value and efficacy of His name. " Who is He that condemneth ? It is Christ that died, yea rather, that is risen again, who is even at the right hand of God, who also maketh intercession for us" (Rom. viii. 34.) No vail now intervenes to hinder our approach into God's presence; and not only have we access with boldness into the holiest through the blood, but there is also "an High Priest over the house of God," who has living active sympathies, ever presenting on our behalf a sweet fragrance of holiness and purity before the throne of grace. Well, therefore, may the word of exhortation be, " Let us draw near with a true heart, in full assurance of faith. (Heb. x, 19-22.)

THE TIMES OF BURNING INCENSE.

Twice a day was the holy perfume to ascend fresh before the Lord. (Exod xxx. 7.) " And Aaron shall burn thereon sweet incense every morning: when he dresseth the lamps he shall burn incense upon it And when Aaron lighteth the lamps at even, he shall bum incense upon it ; a perpetual incense before the Lord throughout your generations. " Reference has already been made, whilst treating of the Candlestick, to these two periods of time, evening and morning. It only remains to be observed that the object of burning incense at these two seasons was, that the fulness of fragrance might perfume the Sanctuary during the ministration of the priest at the Candlestick. When the Lord returned to the glory and joy of the Father's presence above, having accomplished His work on earth, He entered " the better Tabernacle," not for Himself, not on His own account, but as the head and representative of the Church which He had loved, and for which He had died. The light of the Sanctuary then shone forth with its perfect seven-fold lustre; and at the same time that there was thus presented to God a blessed and living witness of the glory and perfectness of that Church which He had loved, and chosen in Christ before the foundation of the world, a fragrant perfume also ascended on its behalf. For, notwithstanding the heavenly calling of the saints, in union with the Lord, yet their real condition of weakness and failure on earth needed the ceaseless living power of His intercession. The golden Altar rolled forth its perpetual cloud of incense during the night, while the lamp shone out with all its 'perfect light And again, at the close of this night of darkness and evil, when the day is just about to dawn, and Christ will present the Church in all its full and undimmed radiance before God in heaven, the last fragrant cloud of perfume will ascend on its behalf; the full value of His intercession, " saving to the very uttermost," will be manifested ; and the saints will be presented in His glory faultless, because of the preciousness of Him in whom they are accepted, and fully perfumed with all the sweet spices. There are two beautiful little scenes in the Canticles, which point onward to that happy time: "Who is this that cometh out of the wilderness like pillars of smoke, perfumed with myrrh and frankincense, with all powders of the merchant?" (iil 6.) And, " Who is this that cometh up from the wilderness, leaning upon her beloved?" (viiL 5.) The bride is here represented coming up out of the wilderness, her tedious journey, her toils and dangers at an end, and entering her rest in triumph, like pillars of smoke, covered with all the fragrance and varied perfumes of the merchant. The barren and waste howling desert has been to her the very garden whence the spices might flow out The soil least adapted, apparently, to produce such perfumes has t>eeh found the most fertile place for their development: for the graces and sweetness of Christ flourish best in scenes of trial, conflict, and danger. His bride will be found, at the close of her wilderness journey, to come up out of the trying and wearisome path covered with all His fragrance, perfumed with all His sweet powders. The other little verse also presents her emerging from the same perilous and toilsome path, "leaning upon her beloved;" sustained alone by Him, and brought up out of the wilderness in safety alone by His strength ; conscious of her need of dependence on His arm, even in the very last step of the way, and never more trusting in His care and power than when taken by Him forever out of the scene of her trial, and placed, perfumed with all His fragrance, in the glory.

THE INCENSE.

And the Lord said unto Moses, Take unto thee sweet spices, stacte, and onycha, and galbanum ; these sweet spices with pure frankincense : of each shall there be a like weight : and thou shalt make it a perfume, a confection after the art of the apothecary, tempered together, pure and holy : and thou shalt beat some of it very small, and put of it before the testimony in the tabernacle of the congregation, where I will meet with thee : it shall be unto you most holy. And as for the perfume which thou shalt make, ye shall not make to yourselves according to the composition thereof: it shall be unto thee holy for the Lord. Whosoever shall make like unto that, to smell thereto, shall even be cut off from his people. (Exod. xxx. 34-38.)

Three sweet spices are here mentioned, "stacte, onycha, and galbanum," the names of which nowhere else occur in Scripture ; neither is there any apparent meaning in the Hebrew words thus translated, so as to lead our souls to any particular truth intended to be typified by them. The perfumes are unknown to us. They may have been selected on that very account; in order thereby to designate a sweetness and fragrance not appreciable to human sense but understood and valued alone by God. Who is able to enumerate the varied graces of Christ? or who can estimate their value? Our souls may and do indeed say, " He is precious;" the fragrance of His sweet perfumes is wafted towards us ; but our thoughts are poor, our words and expressions weak, when we seek to pourtray the beauties and excellencies of His person. All, however, has been presented to God ; every varied grace has yielded its sweet odour to Him ; and He has delighted in, and appreciated each perfume, as from time to time it has been developed in the thoughts and ways of His Son.

To these three unknown spices pure frankincense was added; of each there was to be " a like weight ;" the four ingredients were to be skilfully mingled together, " a confection after the art of the apothecary, tempered together, pure and holy." It has been truly observed by another, " that there was no unevenness in Christ, nothing salient 'in His character, because all was in perfect subjection to God, and had its place, and did exactly its service, and then disappeared." 2 Just so these perfumes which formed the incense were of even weight; no one preponderated over the other; varied as each was, yet one did not overpower another; but each lent its one peculiar fragrance to the whole, and one sweet cloud went up, curiously compounded of various scents — sweet as to each ingredient that composed it, and most sweet as to its combined odour. How true a type does this afford of the character of the blessed Lord! Grace, mercy, righteousness, truth, all had their place in Him, and gave their fragrance to each thought, word, and action. There was no preponderating feature in His character, so as to overpower or eclipse other graces : all was perfect, and of even weight Righteousness was not overpowered by mercy ; holiness and love were not opposed ; all were tempered together, and could blessedly mingle ; a will in subjection to God could skilfully combine every varied fragrance. And when He acted or spake, all were present: the sweet spices, marvellously compounded together, sent forth their one full and blended perfume. In men it is just the reverse: they have features of character that become prominent, and thereby distinguish one man from his fellow; the very names and epithets bestowed on mere human beings are proofs of this. Even that which is naturally sweet and lovely is not held in an even balance. Mercy is applauded at the expense of justice; charity is advocated to the sacrifice of truth; all is uneven and distorted. But in Christ every grace had its due proportion, and its right place.

Some of this sweet compound was to be beaten very small and put before the testimony. The object of finely pounding the incense was in order that its fragrance might be the more developed, and to evidence the fact that each minute fragment had all the varied perfumes of the whole. So, was it in respect of Him to whom this incense points? It was not only on great occasions that the graces of His character manifested themselves; neither was it effort, or the force of circumstances, that produced them: in the smallest as well as greatest action, all that was well pleasing to God was developed. True indeed, the last wondrous act of obedience unto death, even the death of the cross, yields " the hands full of incense ; " but in every previous scene, in every little detail of life, all was also present The varied circumstances through which it pleased the Father that His beloved Son should pass have each in their turn called forth a holy and pure and sweet perfume, which has sanctified each scene, and made the most trivial action to become precious and pleasing to God. The more, under the guidance and teaching of the Holy Spirit, we ponder over the minutest sayings and actions of the Lord, the more shall we be lost in wonder and praise at the combined perfection of grace, wisdom, and truth manifested by this blessed One in all His paths below.

The prevailing odours which this incense exhaled, when its various ingredients had been tempered together, are expressed in those words, "pure, holy" Together with all the sweetness exhibited in the ways of Christ, and the grace and love displayed by Him, so attractive to the poor weary soul, there ever ascended also to God the fragrance of perfect purity and holiness. In the spontaneous out flowings of l}is gracious character, no motive intruded for His own glory or self-exaltation. The very compassion of His heartbeat in unison with the will and purposes of God. When weary and thirsty at the well, He rejoiced in pouring into the heart of a poor sinful woman words of life and healing; still He adds, "My meat is to do the will of Him that sent me, and to finish His work." (John iv. 34.) He tastes this joy, because it is in accordance with the will of God. And when about to lay down His life for the sheep, because of His deep and boundless love for them, He yet speaks of that act as in obedience to a commandment He had received of the Father. (John x. 18.) Here was purity, unmingled with one particle of human taint — motives that may be sifted, and most minutely scrutinized, and which will be found altogether fragrant, and free from the slightest shade of that selfishness and independence of God which so pervade even our best and fairest actions. What holiness also was manifested in the exercise of all His grace! Does sin lose in our estimate any of its evil or corruption though we may hear Him pardon the sinner? Did the poor slave of sin feel less her fearful guilt when she heard those gracious words, " Neither do I condemn thee; go and sin no more"? Or did the woman "which was a sinner" forget the holiness of Him whose feet she had washed with her tears, and wiped with the hairs of her head, though she received from His lips that blessed sentence, "Go in peace"? Surely, in reading such histories of the Lord, our souls are filled with a secret consciousness that we are "on holy ground;" and whilst we rejoice at the spontaneous and rich out- flowings of such mercy, we dare not for a moment trespass on the grace that could so readily pardon; but are arrested rather by the purity and holiness of Him who had power on earth to forgive sins, at the very moment that His love and pity for the poor ruined sinner so manifest themselves. The blended perfumes of the sweet incense ascend, " a confection tempered together— pure, holy."

The precept, " And thou shalt put of the incense before the testimony in the tabernacle of the congregation, where I will meet with thee," was fulfilled by putting incense on the golden Altar. 3 Thus directly before the throne of grace, in the presence of Him who is light, and in whom there is no darkness at all, the Lord Jesus as our High Priest offers a ceaseless intercession; deriving its value and power from the eternal glories of His person. " Because of the savour of thy good ointments, thy name is as ointment poured forth." (Cant i. 3.) Not only has the blood of atonement made peace, and caused all wrath and vengeance to pass away forever, but the value of that precious blood is still maintained in all its freshness and cleansing, by our great High Priest His intercession perpetuates all that is precious, ever causing the sweet savour of His name to abide before God on our behalf; and saving " to the uttermost," or, as it might be rendered, " on to the very end, those that come unto God by Him" Salvation, once commenced, rolls on unchecked to its full consummation in the glory. Jesus carries forward, to the termination of our path here, the perfect and abiding value of all His blessed work. We boast not a mere temporary deliverance; it is not a fluctuating completeness in which we stand ; the living presence, power, and value of Christ before God ever attest our full and eternal salvation. No ill savour of our failures or weaknesses can intrude to hinder our blessing, where the cloud of incense rolls forth its sweet fragrance : the heart of God can there rest respecting us; for, under the shelter of all the grace and holiness of Christ, He views us from off the throne of mercy; and, " perfumed with all powders of the merchant," we have full and confident access at all times into the Sanctuary. It is true that Satan, with restless malice, accuses the brethren day and night before God (Rev. xii. 10); and oftentimes there may be valid ground for his accusations; but "we have an advocate with the Father, Jesus Christ the righteous." He presents a sufficient answer to every plea. He is our " interpreter " with God, one among a thousand, who can show on our behalf uprightness : one who is able to unravel the mystery of God's justice, and our salvation ; who can vindicate holiness, and yet cover our every defilement The presence and power of Christ in the glory for us are results of His wondrous finished work on the cross. On the ground of atonement, effected through the shedding of blood, the Incense Altar yearly took its stand. (Exod. xxx. 10; Lev. xvi. 18, 19.) So the present living service of Christ is the telling out, in God's presence, all His own fragrance, which was so fully manifested in His obedience unto death; and all the priestly offices He bears are so many proofs of the dignity and glory of Him who shed His blood upon the cross. He who is our advocate, and our great High Priest, is also " the propitiation for our sins." No imitation of this holy perfume was to be made. " Ye shall not make to your- selves according to the composition thereof: it shall be unto thee holy for the Lord. Whosoever shall make like unto that, to smell thereto, shall even be cut off from his people." There are many attempts made to follow Christ, and to imitate Him, which spring from the desire to gratify self, and to have something of our own which we may admire, and which may quiet and give rest to the soul. Thus, how much of what passes for Christian grace and sweetness is really but a spurious fabrication of the human heart, for its own self-exaltation, and the feeding of its own vanity! An apparent austerity passes under the name of holiness ; a seeming lowliness gets the credit of humility; a smoothness or liberality, which speaks well of all, is called charity; and many an act which is attributed to self-denial nourishes the flesh instead of resisting it. These are perfumes which men make for themselves, to gratify their own hearts; they are not like the incense of the Sanctuary, all for God, all presented to Him. Self-had no place in the ways of the blessed Lord, He courted not, but shrunk from, the applause of men. May we glory in nothing else but in Him, and not manufacture, as it were, perfumes to smell thereto, to nourish self-complacency, or to gratify our own hearts ; but may whatever we do, as the saints of God, whether in word or deed, be alone to His glory !

It may be seen, on reference to many passages of Scripture, that it was considered a high act of priestly service to present incense on the Altar. "And to the office of Eleazar, the son of Aaron the priest, pertaineth the oil for the light, and the sweet incense," &c. (Num. iv. 16.) "They (the tribe of Levi) shall teach Jacob thy judgments, and Israel thy law: they shall put incense before thee, and whole burnt- sacrifice upon thine Altar." (Deut xxxiiL 10.) "And did I choose him out of all the tribes of Israel to be my priest, to offer upon mine altar, to burn incense, to wear an ephod before me?" (1 Sam. ii. 28.) " But Aaron and his sons offered upon the altar of the burnt-offering, and on the Altar of Incense, and were appointed for all the work of the place most holy, and to make an atonement for Israel." (1 Chron. vi. 49.) "Behold, I build an house to the name of the Lord my God, to dedicate it to Him, to burn before Him sweet incense." (2 Chron. ii. 4.) "And they (the priests) burn unto the Lord, every morning and every evening, burnt-sacrifices and sweet incense." (2 Chron. xiii. 11.) Indeed, the intervention of a priest was necessary, if an Israelite would offer anything to the Lord; for it pertained to the priests alone to minister at the altars, and to draw nigh to God in the holy places of His Tabernacle. But now the true worshipper of God is identical with the priest; the poor sinner, who is washed in the blood of the Lamb, is also made a king and a priest (Rev. i. 5, 6.) The whole family of God compose the royal priesthood; so that it is alike in the power of every believer to draw nigh, even into the Holiest, and to offer spiritual sacrifices acceptable to God by Jesus Christ (Heb. x, 19-24; 1 Peter ii. 5, 9; Rev. v. 8.) All worship, prayer, or praise is a priestly service, and appertains alone to those who have been redeemed by Christ The prayers of such ascend like incense (Psalm cxli. 2), for they are perfumed with the name of Christ; and the fragrance of His intercession renders all sweet and holy before the Lord. (Rev. viii. 3.) We have a striking instance, in the history of Uzziah, of the watchful jealousy of God, that none unsanctioned by Him might intrude into the priest's office. (2 Chron. xxvi.16-19.) He was one who had run well in the early part of his reign, as long as he had a wise counsellor in Zechariah; but when he was strong, his heart was lifted up to his destruction. He took upon himself the service of the priesthood and presuming on the favour and prosperity he had already found at the hands of the Lord, he ventured to offer incense upon the Altar, which alone pertained to the priests. What should have been the place of communion with God, became to him the place where the fearful corruption of the flesh was manifested to its full extent. In the very act of presenting incense, "the leprosy even rose up in his forehead before the priests in the house of the Lord, from beside the Incense Altar. And Azariah, the chief priest, and all the priests looked upon him, and behold, he was leprous in his forehead, and they thrust him out from thence; yea himself hasted also to go out, because the Lord had smitten him." This attempt to serve the Lord only brought out the more the secret evil that was lurking within. A leprosy of the very worst kind (Lev. xiii. 44) showed itself; and instead of being fit for the presence of God, he was thrust out as one "utterly unclean." Is there not in this a solemn warning for those who, not called of God, and not washed in the blood of Christ, yet assume the place of worshippers before Him ; and, like Cain of old, with sin unatoned for " lying at the door," think they may take the place of believers, or seek to render God propitious by some spiritless worship or offering that they present? All such attempts only end in a more fearful manifestation of the evil of the flesh in His presence. The person must be first clean, before he can render acceptable service to the Lord. The blood of the Lamb, and the anointing of the Holy Spirit, must be first known and applied, before any true worship can be presented to God. All endeavours to approach without this only make more apparent the desperate leprosy of the nature : a leprosy not showing itself in the ordinary outbreaks of evil, but in its worst form, as appreciated by a priestly eye; a leprosy of the head — the mind, the understanding darkened, the power of reason perverted, and pride of intellect assuming a title to draw near to God ; instead of the poor ruined sinner, conscious of his utter vileness, seeking first mercy and grace through the precious blood of Christ. In order to be a servant of God there must be freedom from sin, through the death of the Lord Jesus. (Rom. vi 22.) It is not his service to his new master that frees a man from his former one ; but death alone, the death of Christ, sets the sinner at liberty from the thraldom of the flesh ; and new life, and the power of the Spirit, enable him to obey and bring forth fruit unto God. May our souls' value and stand fast in the blessed liberty wherewith Christ hath made us free; and may many a poor leper heard the gracious words of Him who alone could say, " I will — be thou clean!"

In Luke i. 8-n, we read of Zacharias offering incense, and the people praying without at the time of incense. This period for united prayer seems to have been selected by the Jews, from some secret consciousness of the fitness of such a season, whilst fragrance was going up from the golden Altar to God, for supplication on the part of His people respecting their wants. The contrast to believers is exceedingly beautiful. Our High Priest does not at stated intervals, morning and evening, present incense, but He ever liveth to make intercession for us. (Heb. vii. 25.) " He maketh intercession for us." (Rom. viii. 34.) The consequence is, that the hours of prayer of the believer are not only at certain seasons, but "praying always, with all prayer and supplication in the Spirit, and watching thereunto with all perseverance and supplication for all saints." (Eph. vi 18.) "Continue in prayer and watch in the same with thanksgiving." (Col. iv. 2.) "Continuing instant in prayer." (Rom. xii. 12.) Our access into the Holiest is always open, and the sweet savour of the name of Jesus, and the very person of the Lord" Himself, are ever our fragrant memorial in the presence of God.

NOTES TO THE ALTAR OF INCENSE.

1 In the usual pictorial illustrations of the Tabernacle, the Altar of Incense is represented as standing between the Table and Candlestick, on a line with them, close up to the vail. The author, however, believes that its proper position was about midway in the holy place, between the vail and the Tabernacle door. It will be found, on comparing the portions of Scripture which refer to the placing and covering the Incense Altar, that it was placed last, and covered up last, in the Tabernacle. Whereas, if its position had been between the Table and Candlestick, it would have been deposited and covered in due order after the Table, and before the Candlestick. The path, also, of the high priest lay by this Altar, when he went to light or dress the lamps, which would imply that he met it first in his entrance into the Sanctuary.

* This extract is taken from a tract entitled " The Types of Leviticus," to which the reader is referred for much rich and blessed truth respecting the person and work of the Lord. a It has been stated above that the place of the Incense Altar was directly in the way up to the Ark, and that this position was equivalent to its

being placed " before the Ark of the Testimony? Incense, therefore, put on this altar was placed "before the Testimony? Some, in reading this passage in Exodus, have supposed that some of the incense, unburnt, was kept in the Holiest before the Ark. But we shall nowhere find this to have been done by Moses or the priests; nor was incense ever presented to God without being burnt. It will be found that the only way in which the precept was fulfilled was by placing incense on the Altar, as Moses did (Exod. xl. 27), when he accomplished all the commands of God respecting the Tabernacle and its furniture.

• # * In the enumeration of the vessels of the Tabernacle, in Heb. ix. 1-5, no mention is made of the Incense Altar. The reason of this omission seems to be, that the truths mainly treated of in the chapter are those connected with the great day of atonement, when incense was not burnt on the golden Altar, but was carried within the vail, and placed on burning coals in a golden censer directly before the Ark. The golden censer took the place of the Incense Altar on that day, as to the burning of the incense in it; and it is enumerated consequently in the 9th of Hebrews, amongst the vessels of the Tabernacle, as placed in the Holiest. The vail which divided between the Holiest and holy place being now typically rent (Matt, xxvii. 51 ; Heb. x. 20), the Incense Altar sends forth its holy cloud unhindered, directly before the Mercy Seat. Our access is also into the Holiest, where our great High Priest ministers.

THE LAVER.

Exod. xxxviii. 8. — And he made the laver of brass, and the foot of it of brass, of the looking-glasses of the women assembling, which as- sembled at the door of the tabernacle of the congregation.

Exod. xxx. 17-21. — And the Lord spake unto Moses, saying, Thou shalt also make a laver of brass, and his foot also of brass, to wash withal : and thou shalt put it between the tabernacle of the congregation and the altar, and thou shalt put water therein. For Aaron and his sons shall wash their hands and their feet thereat : when they go into the tabernacle of the congregation, they shall wash with water, that they die not ; or when they come near to the altar to minister, to burn offering made by fire unto the Lord : so they shall wash their hands and their feet, that they die not : and it shall be a statute for ever to them, even to him and to his seed throughout their generations.

WE have now arrived at the two principal vessels of the "court of the Tabernacle," namely, the Laver and the Altar of Burnt-offering. Another metal, brass, entered into their composition. Gold was entirely confined to the covered holy places, and to the vessels which stood therein; whilst silver and brass were employed in the construction of the outer court, and the vessels of service which were set there. This latter metal seems intended to typify firmness, solidity, incor- ruptibility, and power of endurance; whereas the gold, as we have seen, has reference rather to glory and costliness. We read of "gates of brass" (Psalm cvii. 16), "bars of brass" (1 Kings iv. 13), and "fetters of brass" (Judg. xvi. 21), as expressive of great strength and indestructibility. In the visions, also, of the Son of man (Dan. x. 6; Rev. i. 15), his feet are like "polished brass," in order to represent the power and strength of Him to whom all judgment has been committed. In the brass of the Laver and the Altar, our thoughts are directed to that firmness of purpose, and divine power of endurance, which were manifested in Christ, as bearing the weight of God's wrath and judgment on behalf of sinners. " He endured the cross, despising the shame." (Heb. xii. 2.)

The Layer forms a remarkable exception to all the other vessels of the Taber- nacle, inasmuch as it was not, strictly speaking, used for priestly service at all. True indeed, the priests were to "wash their hands and their feet thereat;" but no sacrifice or offering was presented, no sweet savour ascended, no ministration God-ward was there affected. Its purpose was to remove that which would have disqualified for service, its aspect being exclusively towards the priests — a fact which itself affords a clue as to the interpretation of this type ; for we shall find, as we further pursue the subject, that the Laver presents to us a figure of Christ, not in any priestly office now in the presence of God for us, but as the one by whose finished work, and in whom, we have ourselves been made priests unto His God and Father.

The brazen mirrors, used by the women " assembling at the door of the Taber- nacle of the congregation," were the materials of which the Laver was formed. 1 The mirror reflects back an image of ourselves; and it is used either to assist in adorning our persons, or to display to our own eyes our natural beauties or defects. If we had any real comeliness — if any beauty of nature yet remained on which we might gaze with complacency, and which might justly raise our self-esteem— then indeed the mirror might be retained and used with profit and satisfaction. But if corruption has taken the place of comeliness, and "from the sole of the foot even unto the head there is no soundness; but wounds, and bruises, and putrifying sores;" — if our nature is depraved from its very source, so that we have been "shapen in iniquity" — then the sooner we cease to contemplate ourselves — the sooner we lose sight of our own reflection, and looking away from self, rest our eyes on Him with whom we have been buried, and in whom we have been quickened and raised from the dead, the happier we shall be, and the holier will be our walk through the otherwise defiling paths of this world. Having once for all thoroughly learnt what we are by nature, we shall cease to look at ourselves, either with the vain hope of discovering some features of beauty in which we might rest with satisfaction, or to be disgusted afresh with the evil and loathsomeness which a true picture of self cannot fail to exhibit.

It may be observed that the complete ruin of human nature was never distinctly enunciated in the law. The types themselves all fall short of depicting this great fact We do indeed find some obscure intimations, which we are now able, through the perfect light of revelation in the New Testament, to follow out; and we can perceive that they inevitably lead to the conclusion of the entire fall of man — body, soul, and spirit But the declaration of this sad truth was not made in all its present distinct- ness till He came, in " the fulness of the time," who was Himself to be the beginning of a new race of men. Accordingly, we find that the sin-offerings in Leviticus refer to certain actual breaches or transgressions of the law, and do not directly teach the fact of the nature of the sinner being depraved. Leprosy also, one of the types which perhaps approaches most nearly to " sin in the flesh," could only be dealt with when some clear and palpable tokens of corruption were manifested to the senses. Contact with death and uncleanness would defile the Israelite; but he was nowhere taught in the law, that those things which proceed "out of the heart" are really the things which pollute the man. (Matt. xv. 18—20.) If the law had once plainly declared the complete and irremediable ruin of the whole man, it could not have been given consistently with itself; it would have been self-contradictory. For of what avail would it be to command righteousness by man's own efforts, if the same word declared his entire impotence and inability to be righteous? How could a physician propose a remedial process, if at the same time he pronounced the patient incurable? One of the purposes of God in giving the law was, by means of its commandments, to bring out into open manifestation the thorough ruin of the flesh. By the law, therefore, "the offence abounded" (Rom. v. 20); "sin became exceeding sinful" (Rom. vii. 13); sin was detected, and the secret springs of the heart's evil laid bare (Rom. iil 20 ; vii. 7, 8) ; the Jew (the best man in the flesh) as well as the poor outcast Gentile has become " guilty before God." It was needful that such a condition of evil should be manifested, in order that grace and faith in Jesus

Christ might be brought in, and righteousness, life, and salvation in Him might triumph. The law served as a test of man's powers, and of man's heart .The pool of Bethesda offered healing to any that had strength to use it: to an impotent man it presented only a tantalizing hope that could never be realized. He might indeed have learnt thereby his own thorough impotence, instead of vainly hoping for power to reach the healing waters; but that was all that he could have obtained from the pool. For it is clear, that if the power to step into it had been his, then he might have done without it altogether : he would not have required its transient virtues, seeing he would already have ceased to be impotent before seeking its aid. So, in respect to the law: one who had power to obey and keep its precepts would not have needed its restraints or promises, for he would have possessed righteousness and life at the very outset. The law then did not directly instruct respecting the entire ruin of the flesh, though one of its chief objects was to make manifest that fact; and there are allusions incidentally mingled with its teaching, from which it may now be inferred. In the type before us we trace a kind of hint as to the uncomeliness of the flesh, in the fact that the women (the fairest portion of mankind) gave up their mirrors ; but even here it is the mere outward appearance, and not the hidden man of the heart that is alluded to.

Blessed instruction may be gathered from the circumstance, that the women " assembling at the door of the Tabernacle' 1 were those whose mirrors were fashioned into the Laver. They had come to the place where the Lord dwelt, and they had probably intended to adorn themselves to their utmost, by the aid of their mirrors, in order to appear before Him in all the beauty they could display; but His presence had dispelled all these visions of their own comeliness, and had made them conscious that it were vain to attempt to please Him by any adornments of the flesh. They therefore stand before Him just as they are : they gather a knowledge of themselves at the door of the Tabernacle more true than even the mirrors could give them : these looking-glasses are consequently laid aside, and the Laver, with its purifying waters, is substituted for them. We find holy men of old learning the truth of the real condition of the flesh much in the same way. Job was a religious man, and perfect in his outward walk, but he little knew the realities of many truths that his head had learnt and his lips uttered : he little knew how truly corrupt he was in heart, though he could at times declare the weak and unclean condition of man ; but when at length he is brought into the presence of God, then the whole truth of his own corrupt nature bursts upon him : " I have heard of thee by the hearing of the ear : but now mine eye seeth thee : wherefore I abhor myself, and repent in dust and ashes." (Job xlii. 5, 6.) Isaiah had prophesied, and had declared the ruined state of the whole Jewish nation ; but he had been a mere spectator of it, till he sees a vision of the glory of the Lord ; and then he finds he is himself " a man of unclean lips," as well as dwelling in the midst of a people of unclean lips. (Isa. vi. 5.) Daniel, the " man greatly beloved," exclaims, " My comeliness is turned in me into corruption," when he saw in a vision one like unto Him that appeared to John in the Revelation. And Peter is convicted in his own conscience of being " a sinful man," when the miracle at the lake of Gennesaret suddenly makes him realize that he is in the presence of the Lord. (Luke v. 8.) In all these instances there is the discovery of sclfy brought with power to the soul, not by denunciations of judgment, nor by any open manifestation of sin, but by the conscious presence of the Lord. God's estimate, and therefore the real condition of the flesh, is learnt, and it is learnt also where He is manifested, who has made a full provision for the entire cleansing of the whole man.

It is needful to remember that self-contemplation effects no change: could the real condition of the soul be traced as accurately as the looking glass reflects an image, yet a man would not thereby be benefited. Gazing constantly at the mirror could never alter or improve one feature of the countenance, or wash away one stain of defilement It is not only necessary that a man should know himself, but that he should also know a way in which he may escape from himself. A poor outcast leper had with muffled lips to pronounce the mournful words "unclean, unclean" — true record of his state — but his leprosy was not thereby lessened. The mirror must lead to the Laver; and God has provided a cleansing bath, to which the poor sinner, conscious of his misery, may at once turn and wash away his sins. But in order that a defiled person may be truly cleansed and rendered fit to approach God, two things are needful : the flesh itself, with all its outward filth and inward sources of corruption, must be purged away, and a new existence, a new life be imparted. The Lord Jesus speaks of these things to Nicodemus, in John iii. This Pharisee came to Jesus " by night," for he had a reputation to lose ; he had whereof to glory in the flesh, being according to human estimation a righteous man ; as such, he had become a ruler of the Jews, a master of Israel. He had not rightly used the mirror to discover his real condition; or, if he had, he had gone his way, and straightway forgotten what manner of man he was. He knew not that he was a lost sinner, and consequently, he knew not Christ as the Saviour — the cleansing Laver. He recognized the Lord only as " a teacher come from God) " and came to Him for instruction, not for salvation, conscious that he had something yet to learn, but ignorant that he was totally corrupt He therefore looked upon Christ as one who was only going to add something to the law of Moses, instead of owning Him as the living source of grace and truth. The Lord at once declares the great and startling truth, " Verily, verily, I say unto thee, except a man be born again, he cannot see the kingdom of God." Here indeed was the faithful mirror held up to man, which proved that no instruction in righteousness, no law of commandments, could set or keep him right ; but that he was so corrupt, so fallen, that he needed a new beginning — a new existence. Nicodemus knew nothing superior to the flesh, — nothing' more comely, — and he was unacquainted therefore with any other birth than that after the flesh : " How can a man be bora when he is old ? can he enter the second time into his mother's womb, and be bora ? " The Lord then states the necessity of a Laver: — " Verily, verily, I say unto thee, Except a man be born of water and of the Spirit, he cannot enter into the kingdom of God. That which is born of the flesh is flesh ; and that which is born of the Spirit is spirit" Here it is declared, again with the double Amen of God, that two things are needed, — a birth " of water" and of " the Spirit? — a birth in which a com- plete cleansing process shall take place, and in which also a life of the Spirit shall be communicated. Man must be born again ; and in entering into life the second time, there must be a provision made for the entire and eternal cleansing away of all that appertained to his previous existence in the flesh : there must be a bath which should also be a birth place : washing and a new life must be combined. To enter the second time into his mother's womb would effect no change, for " that which is born of the flesh is flesh : " could a man be thus born again ten times over, it would work no alteration in him ; he would still remain the corrupt offspring of corrupt parents. Neither would any remedial process effect any improvement; the flesh under the best discipline could never be converted into spirit: that which is born of the flesh ever remains flesh. The teaching and discipline even of God towards it would not alter its root of evil. Israel was a clear proof of this. Educated under His care, hedged in from the rest of mankind by His laws and ordinances, nurtured by Him as His child, and with His oracles in their hands, yet what had been the result? Was the flesh improved? Had these careful and reiterated processes amended it? Christ's presence was an evidence as well as test of their condition. Nicodemus, a very master of Israel, manifested what their flesh still was — self-satisfied, ignorant of God, ashamed of the company of God's own beloved Son : this ruler of the Jews proved the truth of that sad and solemn word, " He came unto His own, and His own received Him not." It was therefore no gradual alteration, no progressive steps in improvement, no mere advance in righteousness, truth, or holiness, which this " teacher come from God " came to propound or assist No ; the flesh — the whole man — must be destroyed : a Laver must be fashioned containing such waters as should completely and forever purge away the very sources of corruption. And such a Laver is Christ crucified : — thence proceeds the cleansing stream which God has Himself provided for the sinner, — and that stream is blood: — "who hath washed us from our sins in His own blood" (Rev. i. 5.) "They have washed their robes and made them white in the blood of the Lamb." (Rev. vii. 14.) The deep waters of death are those alone which God uses to purge withal ; for it is not the washing away the filth of the flesh that could avail, were that possible: the flesh itself must be gone ; the body of sin destroyed. This then is one essential part of the new birth — the destruction of the old nature. Christ crucified is our death unto sin: we have been crucified with Him. In His death God has judged and "condemned sin in the flesh" on our behalf. The billows of wrath have closed for ever over the flesh: in Him we have been plunged into the deep waters of death, in order that the body of sin might be destroyed. This is the being "born of water" But the death of the Lord is also the cleansing womb from whence a new existence springs : out of that death arises life : His grave becomes our birth-place, and the Spirit is the communicator and power of that life, held as it is by us in union with Christ risen, — a life which • is consequently "spirit," as contrasted with flesh. "Now if we be dead with Christ, we believe that we shall also live with him." (Rom. vi. 8.) If Paul could say, " I have been crucified with Christ," he could also add, " Nevertheless I live; yet not I, but Christ liveth in me." (Gal. ii. 20.) And as "that which is born of the flesh is flesh," so " that which is born of the Spirit is spirit." There is no con- version of the one into the other, — no mingling of the two. Blessedly and eternally distinct does the new and everlasting life of the Spirit remain; while the judgment of death abides on all that which is born after the flesh. The Laver is an obscure shadow of these truths of God: its very existence witnessed that all adorning or contemplation of the flesh was at an end; whilst its cleansing waters rendered the priests fit to approach and minister before the Lord.

" And thou shalt put water therein; for Aaron and his sons shall wash their hands and their feet thereat." There are various typical uses of water in Scripture. Sometimes it represents that which cleanses; in other instances, it is an emblem of life. When masses of water, such as the sea, waves, floods, are figuratively employed, it is generally to typify overwhelming judgments or wrath from God. The waters of the Deluge, the waters of the Red Sea, the waters of the deep that encompassed Jonah, have all this latter aspect We need only compare the language of Psalms xlii. And lxix. with Jonah ii., and we shall at once perceive the application of this imagery to the sufferings of the blessed Lord on the cross, under the wrath of God.

Many a type in the Old Testament (and the Laver among the number) declared plainly the truth, that without perfect cleanness no one could draw nigh to God. Hence the diverse washings and purifying in which water was employed. But under the law, the link between the water that cleansed and the waters that overwhelmed in destructive judgment was not seen. In other words, it was not made manifest that cleansing by means of death was God's appointed way. The Lord Jesus was the first and last that came by " water and blood; not by water only, but by water and blood" (1 John v. 6.) He came as the fountain of purity and life to sinful men, but not without blood. It is not only Christ, but Christ crucified that must be known, if the sinner would be cleansed and have everlasting life. Here the fountain of life is combined with the cleansing waters of death and judgment Baptism is a type of these two things — death and resurrection — judgment and life — salvation, but salvation through destruction. The believer, plunged beneath those waters, has vividly set before him the reality that he has been buried with Christ into death, and that he owes his cleanness, and consequent life and fitness for God's presence, to the blessed fact of his having been judged in Christ crucified, and has thereby " suffered in the flesh and ceased from sin." Washing and burial are thus combined, for God's mode of washing the sinner is through death — the death of His Son ; out of whose grave, as typified by the waters of baptism, the believer has been raised, quickened into new life, made clean every whit, and brought into the family of God. " Buried with Him in baptism, wherein also ye are risen with Him through the faith of the operation of God, who hath raised Him from the dead. And you, being dead in your sins and the uncircumcision of your flesh, hath He quick- ened together with Him, having forgiven you all trespasses." (Col. ii. 12, 13.) A type this, not of the washing away of the filth of the flesh, but of the destruction, in judgment, of the flesh itself; at the same time there results the answer of a good conscience towards God, because the old man has been destroyed, and a new and holy life imparted, through the resurrection of Jesus Christ from the dead. (1 Peter iii. a 1.) The Laver, as fashioned by Moses, and containing water, does not directly teach these truths; for the law sought by external cleansings only to render the worshippers fit for God: but in Titus iii. 4-6, we have the great fact of regeneration connected by the Holy Spirit with a vessel of this kind : " But after that the kindness and love of God our Saviour toward man appeared, not by works of righteousness which we have done, but according to His mercy He saved us, by the washing (/aver) of regene- ration, and renewing of the Holy Ghost, which He shed on us abundantly through Jesus Christ our Saviour." Here the "washing," or "laver" as it may be translated, is that of regeneration : the bath of new birth, analogous to the being "born of water" — born out of the death of Christ, wherein all our sins have been washed away — and " the renewing of the Holy Ghost," answers to the being "born of the Spirit;" a new nature — everlasting life — having been imparted through His power ; but besides this, the same blessed Spirit has been "shed on us abundantly." Salvation thus embraces these three unspeakable blessings, the washing from sin in the death of Christ, the communication of a new existence through the action of the Holy Ghost, and the pouring out that same Spirit to be the power, strength, and sustainer of the believer in his walk and service towards God.

One solemn lesson the Laver was well calculated to teach, namely, the holiness of that God to whom the priests were permitted to approach. A little imperceptible dust, unavoidably contracted in their path through the wilderness, was sufficient to render them unfit for His service, and would have exposed them to destructive judgment, had they attempted to minister before Him without its having been previously cleansed away: "When they go into the tabernacle they shall wash with water, that they die not; or when they come near to the altar to minister, to burn an offering made by fire unto the Lord, so they shall wash their hands and their feet, that they die not, 19 It was not only that gross defilements would unfit them for their ministry, and call down vengeance on their heads, but the slightest contact with an unredeemed world, a speck upon the hand or foot, rendered them obnoxious to the fire of judgment, if they ventured unwashed into the presence of the Lord This may well direct our thoughts to the holiness of that God " with whom we have to do His judgments are not against the great open enormities of vice only, which we see around, or the manifest defilements which we can recognise, but His controversy is with the flesh itself, be its developments what they may : whether from thence have proceeded the open grossnesses of sin, which even men can notice and condemn, or whether there is the evil thought within, in some almost unknown and unnoticed form, still it is the flesh, and in that a man cannot please God; all its desires, motives, and exercises are nothing else than "enmity against Him; for it is not subject to the law of God, neither indeed can be." (Rom. viil 7.)

Any outward contact with death, or, as in this case, the hands and feet accidentally sullied, rendered the priests defiled : with us, before we were converted, it was the inward source of corruption, which no external cleansing could remove, that made us unfit for the presence of God — a corruption that manifested itself in all the varied exercises of thought and imagination which external scenes and associations excited, or which developed itself in the grosser works of the flesh, either actually committed or inwardly cherished. As we read in the Epistle of James, i. 14, 15, "Every man is tempted when he is drawn away of his own lust and enticed. Then when lust hath conceived, it bringeth forth sin; and sin, when it is finished, bringeth forth death." Again, ignorance of the defilement was no proof that it did not exist; the priests were to wash whether they knew themselves to be soiled or not. The Laver was not to be neglected because they might fancy themselves clean. So as to man : whether conscious of it or not, he is unclean and unfit for God; he is not the judge of his own condition, neither is his conscience the true index of his state : God alone is the judge of that; and He has provided the precious blood of Christ, a witness on the one hand of what His estimate is of the sinner's ruin, and on the other, the full and eternal remedy for all that ruin. Lastly, no washing would have sufficed save that Which was conducted at the vessel appointed by God to hold the purifying waters. If, having their eyes partially opened to their unclean condition, the priests had sought to purge themselves at some washing-place of their own construction, instead of at the Laver, they would have exposed themselves as much to the wrath of God as if they had altogether neglected His commands. He had provided a vessel con- structed according to His own will, and which He knew would fit them for His own service. Had they sought another; it would have proved that they either despised His commands or undervalued what He had furnished for their use. In either case they would have been guilty of a direct insult against the holiness, majesty, and wisdom of God. God has lifted up the Son of man on the cross, that cleansing, and life might be the result to everyone that believeth. No process, either instead of faith in the cross, or mingled with it, will avail. If anything in the soul either precedes or follows the cross, as a means of healing, Christ is made of none effect Let even one little ordinance be added, and God is insulted; the soul has fallen from grace. In these days it is not likely that anything would be directly substituted to the exclusion of faith in the blood of the Lamb, as a means of fitting the sinner for the presence of God ; but the great spreading snare of Satan is to suggest some additions to faith in that sacrifice, in order to the sinner's justification. The Laver is not altogether set aside, but some attendant vessels, not commanded by God, are arranged for use around it. But if the soul looks to any process antecedent to faith in Christ crucified as necessary to salvation, or makes any addition to that wondrous cleansing bath, so as to attach value to some subsequent efforts of its own, or some ordinances of God as securing redemption, in either case Christ is made of none effect. It was so with some of the Galatians of old. They had not openly set aside the cross of Christ, but they had added to faith a ceremony as a kind of completion of salvation, and thereby they had spoiled the Gospel; Christ profited nothing; they were bewitched by an evil power; they had fallen from grace. And do we not see this evil extending far and wide at this very time? Are there not around us those on the one hand who preach some gradual steps up to Christ, and on the other those who add ordinances to faith in Jesus as in some sense necessary to salvation? Is not baptism itself made to be a rite admitting the person baptized into a something connected with salvation, or a vehicle of some sort of grace linked on with redemption? And are not even the Lord's people almost afraid to lift a clear and warning voice against this subtle setting aside of the cross? Are not many of the saints of God bewildered on the subject, and consequently slow to cry aloud against this dishonour done to the work and person of the blessed Lord Himself? Would that an energy of the Holy Spirit might arouse the Church of God to cry "anathema" on such as bring in "another Gospel, which is not another, but there be some that trouble, and would pervert the Gospel of Christ" !

The Laver had to be resorted to again and again by the priests ; the cleansing and sacrifices under the law had constantly to be repeated, for the worshippers were never purged thereby; the "conscience of sins" still remained, for the blood of bulls and goats could never take away sins ; the waters of the Laver could never reach the heart All was external, and cleansing never penetrated to the source of corruption. But by the offering of the Lamb of God, those that are sanctified are "perfected forever" The Laver of regeneration has effected a complete putting away of the flesh: through that the believer is at once and for ever "made meet to be partaker of the inheritance of the saints in light." Still indeed the flesh is at work; the conflict between flesh and spirit will ceaselessly continue whilst we are on earth; but the practical victory over evil within, is to be maintained on the ground of the victory already accomplished in Christ for us. We are to mortify our members on the earth, because we have in Christ died to sin, and are risen together with Him. We "have put off the old man," and consequently we are to put on the practical ways of a believer. (Col. iii. 9-12.) We are to walk in the Spirit because we are alive in the Spirit (Gal v. 25.) Here it is that many of the children of God mistake, through want of a clear perception of the great truths of salvation. The teaching of the Spirit of God is (if we may use the expression), from heaven to earth, and not from earth to heaven. He would fix our faith steadfastly on the fact that " old things are passed away, and all things are become new." He would instruct us as to the entire destruction of the flesh in the death of Jesus for us, and in our consequent life and resurrection with Christ risen and glorified ; and having fastened our souls on these blessed facts, and thus rooted and grounded us in Christ, He would then make these truths to be the practical power of our walk and conduct on earth ; so that we come back again to earth from heaven, to walk here below as a heavenly people, following the steps of that blessed one who came forth into the world from the Father. Unhappily too much of the teaching of the present day is of the reverse order —

an attempt to lead to heaven by means of a clean walk on earth, instead of presenting a clean walk on earth as the result of being already " seated in heavenly places in Christ."

THE FOOT.

Whenever the Laver is mentioned, it is always accompanied with this addition, "and his foot." (Ex. xxx. 18, 28; xxxi. 9; xxxv. 16; xxxviii. 8; xxxix, 39; xL 11; Lev. viii. 11.) The word translated "foot" is not the ordinary one but P, which means "a base," or "basis." It was the firm part on which the Laver rested. No provision is made in the Scripture for carrying this vessel : there were no rings or staves attached to it, nor was there any "bar" provided on which i% was to be borne : and in Num. iv., where the other vessels of the Tabernacle and Court are enumerated, and their respective coverings for the march specified, all mention of the Laver is omitted. Taking this fact in connection with its having a "base" whereon it rested, our minds are directed to the thought that this vessel had a definite place on earth ; and that it was not, as far as it was a type, supposed to be moved about during the wilderness journey. Of course, as to fact, it was carried, but all mention of that circumstance is studiously excluded; and in seeking to interpret the type, we must avoid adding to what is recorded: an omission is often pregnant with typical importance. We are hereby apparently instructed in the fixedness and full accom- plishment of the work of regeneration, and that it has its place on earth. The Lord Himself, when instructing Nicodemus in truths connected with regeneration, speaks of them as "earthly things," hrCy€ui (J no. iil 12), things that take place on earth. Christ is the regenerating Laver because of His work on earth; and the fact of regeneration is not connected with any present priestly ministration of the Lord above but is entirely a result of His death and resurrection here below. Besides which, it is while men are here in the flesh that they must, if ever, be born again ; the passing out of this world to another would effect nothing. Could a man be translated from earth to heaven, his corrupt nature would remain unchanged; and the separation of the soul from the body at death improves not the sinner. But when once a man is bora again he has new and everlasting life — he is cleansed fo ever : he has indeed to turn again and again to the cross of Christ for the sustain- ment of his soul, and for power over sin ; he has hourly to remember that the " blood of Jesus Christ cleanseth us from all sin," but he has already received the first great and enduring gift — "eternal life;" and thenceforward the Lord Himself becomes the strength and power of that life : "This life is in His Son." (i John v. n.) " He that eateth me, even he shall live by me." (John vi. 57.)

The apostle, when writing to the Corinthians, though he had to rebuke them for many sins allowed in their midst, yet confidently says, " But ye are washed, but ye are sanctified, but ye are justified in the name of the Lord Jesus, and by the Spirit of our God." (1 Cor. vi. 11.)

THE PLACE OF THE LAVER.

Exod. xl. 7. — And thou shalt set the laver be* I Exod. xl. 30. — And he set the laver between tween the tent of the congregation and the altar. the tent of the congregation and the altar. In the arrangement of the vessels in the Court of the Tabernacle, there seems to be an intention to denote the advance in truth which the soul makes, as it learns in the presence of the Lord, and by the teaching of His Spirit, the vast and varied blessings connected with redemption. We first approach the "gate of the court" and pass through it into the Court of the Tabernacle. " I am the door" said the good Shepherd; " by me if any man enters in he shall be saved, and shall go in and out and find pasture." (John x. 9.) Here is one great truth of salvation learnt — Christ as "the way" through whom the believer enters into God's presence. We next approach the Altar of Burnt-offering, having passed through the gate; the blessed truth of acceptance would here be realized; so that not only is the believer saved from wrath and sin, and a way made for him into the presence of God, but he is accepted accord- ing to all the perfectness and sweet savour of Christ Again, a little further on we find the Laver between the Altar and door of the Tabernacle. At this vessel we are instructed in other truths, namely, as to the cleanness required in those who would serve God, and that He has provided that wherein the very source of evil has been washed away, and whereby the believer, as a new and risen person, is made meet for and has access into the heavenly courts, having a heavenly calling. The door of the Tabernacle may now be entered, the glory and beauty of the risen Lord be known, and the high standing and exaltation of the saint, as united to Him, be appreciated. Thus the progress of the soul of a believer in truth may be gathered from the arrangements of the Court and Tabernacle ; though we must remember that all these blessings are the portion of every believer from the moment of his conversion, however little they may at first be realized. One observation may be made in conclusion, and that with reference to John xiii. The action of the Lord, related in this chapter, of washing the feet of His disciples, has been thought by some to refer to the priests washing at the Laver. This, however, seems hardly to be sustainable ; for the priests were to wash their hands as well as feet: whereas the Lord says, " He that is washed needeth not save to wash his feet." Again, the priests were to wash themselves, and that on pain of death : in John xiii., on the contrary, it is the Lord who washes the disciples, and they are instructed to wash one another's feet Some priestly work of His own towards the believer is hereby manifestly typified ; a service in which the saints themselves may participate. The act seems to refer to His constant watchfulness over His saints, in order that no carnal defilements, which they contract during their path along this world, might render their feet unfit to tread the heavenly courts above, or exclude from conscious fellowship with the Father. The Laver, on the other hand, leads our thoughts to the mode in which our unclean nature itself has been purged away.

NOTES TO THE LAVER.

1 In our version the word "women" is in italics, because it is not found in the original. Some have from this fact supposed that it is wrongly inserted^ and that the mirrors were used by men ; but the Hebrew has the succeeding word " assembling," or " troops," with a feminine termination; from whence it would appear that the English translation is correct. It will be observed that in the

drawing of the Laver which accompanies this exposition, the circular shape in which it is ordinarily represented is not preserved. There is, in fact, no direc- tion given in the Word, either as to the form or dimensions of this vessel ; but it may be inferred that it was not circular, from the fact of the brazen scaffold used by Solomon (2 Chron. vi. 13), which was called by the same name, 'tf 1 ?, being five cubits long, five broad, and three high, and consequently of a rectangular form. It is remarkable that these are exactly the dimensions of the Altar of Burnt-offering, whilst the name Laver is given to this brazen scaffold. Solomon kneeled down on its summit, and spreading forth his hands towards heaven, uttered that beautiful prayer for blessing upon Israel in connection with the temple. May it not be "hereby intimated that the Altar and I<avef are but one vessel, cleansing and acceptance being derived from the same source? And is nòt a time here pre-shadowed when the King and Priest shall, by virtue of His own blessed work, as the basis of His exaltation in glory, call down, with uplifted hands, blessings from heaven upon the head of His ancient people ? The shape of the Altar would have been preserved in the drawing of the Laver, had it not been thought that some confusion between the two might have resulted; and, accordingly, a hexagonal form has been substituted. The " foot" or " base" is represented by the stand on which the vessel containing the water rests.

THE BRAZEN ALTAR

Exod. xxvii. 1-8. — And thou shalt make an altar of shittim-wood, five cubits long, and five cubits broad; the altar shall be foursquare: and the height thereof shall be three cubits. And thou shalt make the horns of it upon the four corners thereof: his horns shall be of the same: and thou snalt overlay it with brass. And thou shalt make his pans to receive his ashes, and his shovels, and his basons, and his fleshhooks, and his firepans: all the vessels thereof thou shalt make of brass. And thou shalt make for it a grate of network of brass; and upon the net shalt thou make four brazen rings in the four corners thereof. And thou shalt put it under the compass of the altar beneath, that the net may be even to the midst of the altar. And thou shalt make staves for the altar, staves of shittim-wood, and overlay them with brass. And the staves shall be put into the rings, and the staves shall be upon the two sides of the altar, to bear it. Hollow with boards shalt thou make it: as it was shewed thee in the mount, so shall they make it.

Exod. xxxviii. 1-5. — And he made the altar of burnt-offering of shittim-wood: five cubits was the length thereof, and five cubits the breadth thereof; it was foursquare; and three cubits the height thereof. And he made the horns thereof on the four corners of it; the horns thereof were of the same: and he overlaid it with brass. And he made all the vessels of the altar, the pots, and the shovels, and the basons, and the fleshhooks, and the firepans: all the vessels thereof made he of brass. And he made for the altar a brazen grate of network under the compass thereof beneath unto the midst of it. And he cast four rings for the four ends of the grate of brass, to be places for the staves.

THE ALTAR OF BURNT OFFERING

THERE are three ways in which this holy vessel is specially designated in Scripture, in order to distinguish it from the Altar of Incense. First, it is emphatically termed "the Altar." (Exod. xxviii. 43; xxix. 12, 44; xxx. 20, &c.) The Hebrew word for altar, has distinct reference to the thought of sacrifice, being derived from a verb signifying to slay or slaughter. Our word altar is from the Latin, signifying high; so that in the English language the true meaning of the original is not expressed. With the sacrifice, and therefore with the Altar, all priestly ministrations, and all acts of worship conducted at the Tabernacle, were inseparably connected. No sin could be atoned for, no praise or thanksgiving could ascend to God, without the intervention of this all-important vessel. The sweet savour of the morning and evening lamb, offered here, sheltered the hosts of Israel, notwithstanding their failures and weaknesses : the Sabbath, completing each week, and giving a type of a rest yet to come, was ushered in with fresh offerings presented on this Altar ; each year and each month, as it rolled round, commenced with additional sacrifices consumed here ; and the feasts, as they recurred, marking annual periods of humiliation or of joy, were celebrated with abundant victims, burnt at this appointed place for a memorial of acceptance before the Lord. Whether an individual Israelite or the assembled congregation approached to worship God, this holy vessel was called into requisition; and the very consecration of the priesthood itself advanced only step by step with the sanctification of this Altar. In fact, the very existence of Israel as a nation, and the life and history of each individual amongst them were in a certain sense linked on with this holy vessel ; for their national deliverance out of Egypt, and their rest in the land, were to be celebrated annually in connection with the place where the burnt-offerings ascended towards God ; and each faithful one amongst them had there to present the first-fruits of all his increase, and the firstlings of his flocks and herds : thus manifestly connecting his prosperity with the sacrifices at the Altar. All this points out the vast importance of this holy vessel and teaches us the reason why it was emphatically called the Altar. And is it not also far more true respecting the Church of God, that to the sacrifice and priesthood of the Lord Jesus, faintly shadowed forth by the Altar and its victims, she owes all her cleanness, her acceptance, and her glory? God's record of the death and resurrection of His Son is the announcement to her of the end of her sins, and the commencement of her life, her purity, and joy. Salvation through the blood of the Lamb, and acceptance in all the unspeakable value of His person, form the very basis of her true and spiritual worship. Every fresh mercy received, and every renewed estimate of her blessings, are celebrated by a recurrence to the " one offering," by which she has been sanctified and perfected forever ; and she enters her rest and glory hereafter with a new song of joy, a fresh shout of exultation, recording again the value of His death, who " hath loved her, and given Himself for her."

Another name by which this vessel is distinguished is " the Altar of Burnt- offering." (Exod. xxx. 28; xxxi. 9; xxxv. 16; xxxviii. 1 ; xL 6, 10, 29; Lev. iv. 7, 10, 18, &c.) Our word burnt-offering hardly expresses the meaning of the original, n^y, olah, which signifies ascending. It is a very appropriate name for this vessel, because all that was there consumed ascended towards God, " an odour of a sweet savour." The word conveys the thought of the blessed acceptance, in which all went up to the Lord, from the fire of this Altar ; and not only so, but that all which was placed there was for the Lord, and for Him alone. There are two principal aspects in which Christ in His death is presented in the types, and in other parts of the Word of God. First, as bearing sin, and dying under the wrath and fearful judgment of God, inflicted upon Him in order that those on whose behalf He* suffered might escape. Accordingly, we read, "Thou shalt make His soul an offering for sin." (Isaiah liii. 10.) " He hath made Him to be sin for us, who knew no sin." (2 Cor. v. 2i.) " God sending His own Son in the likeness of sinful flesh, and for sin, con- demned sin in the flesh." (Rom. viii. 3.) " Who His own self bare our sins in His own body on the tree." (1 Peter ii. 24.) " Christ was once offered to bear the sins of many." (Heb. ix. 28.) The Passover is a leading type of this : Israel in Egypt, oppressed by cruel bondage, slew the lamb, and sprinkled the blood on their door- posts ; the wrath of God was thereby averted from them, and fell only on those who were not under its shelter. The blood of the slain lamb was a witness to God, and token to Israel, that death had already passed upon another in their stead ; and accordingly the sword of vengeance passed over them, and smote them not. Another aspect of the death of Christ is that intended to be conveyed by the burnt-offerings consumed on this Altar. Our thoughts are here directed not so much to Christ as suffering under wrath, as to His holy obedience in death, thus surren- dering Himself and all His powers to God — His mind, His will, and His affections : all were presented, and all offered up to Him in humble and entire devotedness, " an offering of a sweet savour." God delighted in this sacrifice ; He was com- pletely glorified in it ; He searched it according to all the searching judgment of His holiness, of which the fire is a type ; and all was pure and spotless, all was clean and fragrant, even to the very " inwards and all could ascend as a sweet savour, infinitely acceptable and precious to Him. Thus the delight which God had in the offering up of His own blessed Son, and the fragrance of His obedience in death, are the truths mainly pourtrayed by the sacrifices presented on the Altar of Burnt- offering : and as Jesus, in His death, was made sin for us, and bare away our sins forever, so also, according to all the sweet savour of His obedience in death, and according to all the delight the Father has in His Son, in whom He has been thus perfectly glorified, are we accepted of God, and rejoiced over and delighted in by Him. The value of His person, who has on the cross manifested all that was weil- pleasing to God, is the infinite measure of our acceptance. The blood of the paschal lamb was the means of averting wrath, whilst the burnt-offering on the Altar testified of cleanness and perfect acceptance on the part of the offerer. The former repre- sents the death of Christ, as the only way of escape from judgment : the latter again presents to us the same death, but as the means whereby we are made acceptable worshippers before God, and have access into His presence, being estimated accord-ing to all the value of the Lamb slain. Both truths are united in that one sacrifice, though in the types we have often particular aspects separately presented.

The other usual designation for this Altar is " the Altar by the door of the Tabernacle" or rather " tent of the congregation." 1 This expression, " by the door of the Tabernacle," does not necessarily imply that the Altar was close to the door, but it rather refers to the position of this vessel, as standing with immediate reference to the entrance of the Tabernacle. In fact, the Laver stood nearer the door than the Altar, for it was placed " between the tent of the congregation and the altar." (Exod. xl. 30.) As the Altar of Incense was directly on the way into the Holiest, so the place of the Altar of Burnt-offering was immediately fronting the entrance of the Tabernacle. Thus there could be no approach into the presence of God without first passing the place of sacrifice. Acquaintance and intercourse with Him can only be formed through a knowledge of the Lamb slain ; and the way which has been opened for the sinner into the very holiest of all, through the blood of Christ, itself witnesses that there is no other mode of access, no other pathway to God. The death of Christ is at once that which testifies to an open door, at the same time that it forbids any other attempt to reach God. Thus a priest, who desired intercourse with Jehovah in the Tabernacle, must first pass the Altar of Burnt-offering at the door, and enter the holy place under the sweet savour of the lamb, ascending from the fire of the Altar.

THE MATERIALS OF THE ALTAR.

This Altar was made of shittim-wood and overlaid with brass. The wood, as has been before remarked respecting the Ark, Shewbread Table, and Incense Altar, was the chief material of which they were fashioned: the brass added durability and firmness, and the power to sustain the fire.

In again alluding to the person of Christ as God and Man, it is well for us to remember one of old, who, when he desired to turn aside and see the great sight why the bush was not consumed by the fire that burnt within it, was commanded not to draw nigh, but to put off the shoes from off his feet, for he was standing on holy ground. (Exod. iii.) And if that sight was marvellous, and was to be regarded with holy reverence, and not scrutinized with heedless curiosity, truly " God manifest in the flesh" is a great mystery, before which we do well to bow; submitting our reason and understanding to what the Scriptures declare concerning it, without seeking to reduce it to the level of our poor finite comprehension. Two blessed objects were before the Lord when He became Man, which are beautifully connected together in Hebrews ii. : the one was to be the sacrifice, the other to be the priest. Accordingly, we read, " Forasmuch as the children are partakers of flesh and blood, He also Himself likewise took part of the same; that through death He might destroy him that had the power of death, that is, the devil." And again, " It behoved Him to be made like unto His brethren, that He might be a merciful and faithful High Priest in things pertaining to God, to make reconciliation for the sins of the people." Whether, therefore, we contemplate Him as the Lamb of God appointed to be slain, or as the Apostle and High Priest of our profession in the glory, still the blessed truth of His being a man is that which presents itself prominently to our faith, and is one great basis on which the realities of salvation rest ; just as the " incorruptible wood" is one chief component part of the holy vessels. While inseparable, though distinct, is the other great verity as to the person of Christ, namely, that He was " GOD manifest in the flesh," and that His power and excellency as God have rendered effectual and precious all that He has accomplished on earth in death, and all that He still perpetuates in resurrection of blessed service for His saints ; we shall ever find that the Word of God steadily keeps the person of the blessed Lord before us, and does not treat abstractedly of His natures either as God or Man. And this is the one great means of preserving the soul from evil and unholy specu- lations on such a subject It may be well here to notice one erroneous form of expression which is prevalent, relative to the incarnation of the eternal Word ; and that is that Christ assumed a* human nature merely as a kind of casket, in which His divinity was enshrined. The Scripture invariably opposes its statements to this kind of thought. We read in Luke i. 35, " That holy thing which shall be born of thee shall be called the Son of God;" and again, "

The Word was made fleshy and dwelt among us." (John l 14.) He became by incarnation as truly Man, as He is, and from all eternity hath been, God. Humanity was not a mere vestment, veiling for a while the glories of His Godhead. No: He was " God manifest in the flesh," not God enshrined or concealed under its guise. The eye of faith beheld in the " Man of sorrows" the "glory of the only begotten of the Father." And still He is, and ever will be, Man. It is now His very being, while from everlasting to everlasting He is God. How blessedly are these truths combined in two Psalms, quoted in Heb. i. ! Psalm cii. opens with a strain of sorrowful lamentation, which is suddenly arrested by the voice of Jehovah encouraging the Son, reminding Him of His own past acts of greatness and power, when He laid the foundation of the earth, and fashioned the heavens, and the yet future display of His Godhead, when He shall change as a garment the whole face of creation. The utterances of the Man of sorrows are here stayed by assurances of His eternal power and Godhead; the groan of the dying Saviour is recognized as the voice of the Almighty Creator. In the other, Psalm xlv., we have a beautiful contrast with this. The Lord Jesus in resurrection is there addressed as God in the glory: " Thy throne, O God, is for ever and ever! " and then He is immediately recognized as Man: " Thou lovest righteousness, and hatest wickedness: therefore God, thy God, hath anointed thee with the oil of glad- ness above thy fellows." In the former Psalm we have a dying Christ hailed as the eternal Creator, God: in the latter we have the risen Christ acknowledged as God, and then addressed as Man.

THE DIMENSIONS AND PARTS OF THE ALTAR.

The square form of this vessel has been alluded to elsewhere: without now attempting to interpret the typical import of the numbers five and three employed in its measure- ments, two things may be noticed. First, that its dimensions are such that all the other vessels of the Sanctuary could be included within it, and next, that there seems to be a manifest connection between its size and that of the Ark : for on referring to the measurements of the latter, we shall find that the height was one cubit and a half, just half the height of this Altar ; and the length was two cubits and a half, exactly half its length. May not these facts be intended to foreshadow, first, that every priestly ministration is involved in or connected with the death of the Lord Jesus, as every vessel of the Tabernacle was smaller than, and could be included in, the sacrificial Altar ; and, secondly, that intercourse with God is a result from the fact of sacrifice, and is closely connected with it, as the size of the Ark is dependent on the size of the Altar? One great object of God in giving His Son was to establish full and free intercourse with Himself ; so that the sinner, unhindered by his sins, might draw nigh, and might find and taste all the fresh springs of mercy and of love flowing out from God abundantly through Christ Besides the horns, which have been noticed before, there was also connected with this vessel an integral and important part, namely, the brazen grate. It would appear that the Altar itself was a hollow square, without top or bottom ; and that this grate of strong brazen net-work was fastened just half way up the interior, reaching therefore one cubit and a half from the ground, exactly the height of the Mercy seat : 2 to the corners of the grate, which must have pierced the angles of the Altar, four rings were attached, serving as places for the staves. The grate would by its strength prevent the Altar from twisting out of its form when it was moved; and the weight of the whole would be sustained on the rings to which the staves were attached. The word "^P, grate, occurs nowhere else ; it is derived from a root signifying to plait, or twist: the word net-work is also added in the description of the construction of the grate ; and thus this portion of the Altar was formed of strong interwoven bars of brass, which could not be broken. May not this point to that truth connected with the sacrifice of Christ, that there was no escape from the judgment which He came to bear, because no other plan or way of salvation could be devised? The unsearchable wisdom of God could provide no other remedy — could discover no other way of redemption: His only-begotten Son must be delivered up to death, even the death of the cross. The blessed Lord Himself realized this truth in His own soul; for after praying, " O my Father, if it be possible, let this cup pass from me— if Thou be willing, remove this cup from me," He adds, " Nevertheless, not my will but Thine be done." " The Son of

Man must be lifted up;" refuge failed Him, and He was as a victim appointed to the slaughter, for whom there was no escape. The determinate counsel of God, the ruin of man, for which there was no other remedy, the devotedness of His own heart's obedience to the Father, and His deep and boundless love for the Church, acted as so many constraining powers to bind Him to the work : they were like the meshes of brazen net-work which firmly retained the sacrifice on the altar. There is a passage in the Lamentations which seems to express the thought connected with the death of Christ, of its being a net from whence there was no deliverance : " Is it nothing to you, all ye that pass by ? behold, and see if there be any sorrow like unto my sorrow, which is done unto me, wherewith the Lord hath afflicted me in the dsy of His fierce anger. From above hath He sent fire into my bones, and it prevaileth against them: He hath spread a net for my feet; He hath turned me back; He hath made me desolate and faint all day. The yoke of my transgressions is bound by His hand ; they are wreathed, and come up upon my neck ; He hath made my strength to fall ; the Lord hath delivered me into their hands, from whom I am not able to rise up." (Lam. i. 12-14.)

VESSELS ATTACHED TO THE ALTAR.

Five sets of attendant vessels are enumerated as connected with this Altar; and so important and needful were they, that they are described in the midst of the directions for making the Altar itself. They were pans, shovels, basins, flesh-hooks, and fire-pans. The pans, HITp, are elsewhere translated pots and caldrons; here their use is specified to receive the ashes of the Altar, not the flesh of the sacrifices for seething. In Lev. vi. 10, 1 1, a peculiar ordinance is given respecting the removal of the ashes, when these vessels were employed : " And the priest shall put on his linen garment, and his linen breeches shall he put upon his flesh, and take up the ashes which the fire hath consumed with the burnt-offering on the Altar, and he shall put them beside the Altar. And he shall put off his garments, and put on other garments, and carry forth the ashes without the camp unto a clean place." This was a solemn and important ceremony: a peculiar dress was needed for the occasion,

The Holy Vessels and Furniture of the Tabernacle of Israel

and a change of garments occurs in the midst t>F the service. The dress, both on this occasion and on the great day of atonement (Lev. xvl), was made of the same material, namely, linen ; not the same as those of which the garments " for glory and for beauty " were made ; for though our translation also uses the word linen as one of the component parts of those garments, yet in the Hebrew quite another term is employed. The word for " fine linen," of which the curtains, vail, hangings, and priestly garments for glory and for beauty were formed, is ; that for " linen," of which the holy gar- ments for atonement and for removing the ashes were made, is It would appear from this, that there was a kind of analogy between the two ceremonies, and that the action of removing ashes from the Altar had certain characteristics connected with it similar to some of the services on the great day of atonement In seeking to under- stand this type, it will be needful, first, to consider what the ashes are intended to represent. They were the record that all had been consumed on the Altar, and consequently that the offering had been fully accepted and had ascended to God as an odour of a sweet savour : they afford us a type of the Lord in death after He had uttered those most blessed words, " It is finished," and had bowed His head and yielded up the ghost. The priest when taking away the ashes would have the evidence in his hands that the penalty incurred by sin had been met, and the means of a full atonement provided ; he was handling the very record of death, and such a record of it as proved that a complete satisfaction had been rendered to God. His garments were therefore analogous to those of atonement; for he would be contem- plating that which was a speaking witness of complete reconciliation made. To consume the burnt sacrifice to ashes, was equivalent to a full and perfect acceptance of the offering; so, we find it in Psalm xx. 3, " The Lord remember all thy offerings, and accept (or, as the margin correctly renders it, turn to ashes) thy burnt-sacrifice." And when we contemplate the lifeless body of the blessed Lord on the cross, when the soldiers came and found that He was dead already, we seem to be like the priest removing the ashes from the Altar; we mark the wounded side pouring forth the blood and water, — a witness not only that Jesus was dead, but that an atoning and life-giving power was in that death ; God's token also of the full and finished work of His Son. The ashes, having been taken from the Altar, were then to be deposited by its side ; and we learn from Lev. i. 16, that the place of ashes was "on the east part : " here for a while they remained under the eye of God, while the priest was changing his garments. Thus, they were not hurriedly removed out of sight; but even after the fire had fully consumed the victim, this record of the fact still remained before the Lord. This may be intended to mark the deliberateness with which all was ordered by God respecting the death of His Son. His body remained on the cross sometime after death, exposed, indeed, to the idle gaze of the unthinking multitude. But how must the eye of God have rested there? How precious to Him that marred form — how dear to us those ashes! The east, it may be, was chosen for the place of ashes, because thence the bright light of the morning sun arose. The place of death is closely connected with the glory of resurrection; the rising of the Sun of righteousness with healing in His wings only the more casts back the light of the glory upon all that was connected with His death. The priest then changed his garments and put on others not spoken of as priestly. He ceases to exercise any direct ministration, for he had presented the ashes to God, placing them beside the Altar. The testimony as to acceptance was complete ; the sacrifice had been reduced to ashes ; the full record of atonement had been presented, for the ashes were the witness how entirely the work had been accomplished in death ; and now they are carried forth without the camp unto a clean place. This seems a type of the burial of the Lord. He was laid in a new sepulchre, wherein man had never before been laid, and His burial-place was outside the city of Jerusalem, or,' as it is in type, "outside the camp." (Compare Heb. xiii. 11, 12.) This clean place, where the ashes of the Altar were poured out, was also the place where the sin-offerings were burnt (Lev. iv. 12); and so it was as to the Lord's burial, for the place of the tomb was a garden on the very mount where He was crucified : " Now in the place where He was crucified was a garden, and in the garden a new sepulchre." (John xix. 41.) It is deeply interesting here again to see how the Spirit of God combines in the death of Christ the two great aspects of acceptance and judgment. There is a " place of ashes" at the Altar of acceptance, where the record of death is ever the odour of a sweet savour to God ; there is a place, also, where the ashes are poured out, where the burning of the victim speaks of all-consuming wrath. The one is inseparable from the other, though very different truths are taught at each. The burial of the Lord Jesus is a fact definitely marked in prophetic Scripture, and also is one of the articles of our faith: Isa. liii. 9, "And He made His grave with the wicked, and with the rich in His death; " and in 1 Cor. xv. 4, the Apostle, when declaring the great cardinal truths of the gospel which he preached, includes in the enumeration, " And that He was buried." The pans to receive the ashes of the Altar are therefore important vessels. The Lord Jesus Himself, as our Priest, is the one who instructs us by His Spirit in all the truths connected with salvation and glory ; and in contemplating these types, we have to consider that they are not only significant of what has been already fulfilled in the one great antitype, but that they are often tokens to us of the various priestly minis- trations of Christ, now that He is risen, both as towards God on our behalf, and as Himself instructing us in the blessed truths connected with His death, so that we might have fellowship with the Father and with Himself respecting all His finished work.

On referring to Num. iv. 13, we shall find that the ashes were also removed from the Altar before it was covered for the march ; and these vessels were then also used to hold them, as is clear from the fact that they are omitted from the list of the other vessels covered and carried on the Altar. "And his shovels." The four remaining sets of vessels were required for priestly ministration more immediately connected with the Altar; and we therefore find they are called "his shovels/' "his basons," &c. ; whereas the pans before mentioned are not thus designated, but their use is specified, "to receive his ashes." The shovels seem to be intended for removing the fire from the Altar into the censers; for the original, DW, is derived from a root signifying to take away. In Jer. Hi. 19 (margin), they are called "instruments for removing the ashes;" but as the pans were especially appropriated to this use, and as these vessels are called his shovels, thereby connecting them directly with the Altar, it is far more probable that they were employed to fill the censers with burning coals from off the Altar, when fire had to be carried into the holy place. If this be so, these vessels would form a link between the ministration at the two Altars, connecting the presentation of incense inseparably with the coals of fire which had fed upon the burnt-offering. A chain of holy service, commencing with the offering of the lamb at the sacrificial Altar, and closing with the cloud of fragrant perfume filling the Tabernacle, when the golden candlestick was sending forth its sevenfold lustre, would thus be presented to our thoughts; and the complete acceptance of the true worshipper, and the light and fragrance in which he stands to minister in God's presence, would thus be traced up to and connected with that one leading truth, " Christ hath given Himself for us an offering and a sacrifice to God for a sweet-smelling savour." (Eph. v. 2.)

"And his basons." Here the word P*J!P, a vessel for sprinkling, at once directs us to the use of these bowls. They were employed to receive the blood of sprinkling which flowed from the various victims offered at the Altar. It might almost seem superfluous to remind believers in the Lord of the great use and efficacy of the blood ; and yet there is no truth which we need more to retain in our hearts, or to testify with our lips, than the value of the precious blood of Christ. On it depends all our present peace of soul, as well as our hopes of future glory. It is our great weapon against Satan; "They overcame him by the blood of tHe Lamb, and by the word of their testimony" (Rev. xii. 11); it is the means of our justification with God, "being justified by His blood" (Rom. v. 9): the Lord Jesus Himself, that great Shepherd of the sheep, has been " brought again from the dead through the blood of the everlasting covenant " (Heb. xiii. 20); and has entered once for all into the holy places in the heavens, as our great High Priest, by His own blood, having obtained eternal redemption for us. (Heb. ix. 12.)

There are two principal uses of the blood, specified in the Epistle to the Hebrews : first, it was sprinkled to confirm the covenant ; and, secondly, it was the only means of atonement The old covenant was ratified by the blood of calves and of goats, with which Moses sprinkled the book and all the people, saying, " This is the blood of the covenant which God has enjoined unto you."

(Heb. ix. 19, 20.) The new covenant has been established in the blood of Christ, so that the promises of blessing contained therein are eternally and irrevocably sealed to the saints of God. The main term of this blessed covenant, upon which all the other promises included in it depend, is the last, "Their sins and iniquities will I remember no more" (Heb. x. 1 7) ; and this is the result of the shedding of Christ's blood, as the Lord Himself said, in anticipation of His death, when He took the cup, " This is my blood of the new covenant, which is shed for many for the remission of sins." (Matt xxvL 28.) The blood of the burnt-offerings and peace-sacrifices was sprinkled round about upon the Altar seemingly with these two aspects, namely, to present on every side, towards God and towards the people, a record of the remission of sins, and also to confirm afresh all the blessings of favour and acceptance recorded in the offerings burnt as a sweet savour on the Altar. The ratification of blessing was the primary object in these instances, though atonement held necessarily a place in all sacrifices where life was taken. We find a different word used for sprinkling, when the blood of the burnt-offerings and peace-sacrifices is alluded to, from that employed when the blood of the sin-offerings is mentioned. In the former case it is P"K, in the latter A distinction also is preserved between the word used for burning the offerings presented at the brazen Altar, and that used for burning the sin-offerings outside the camp. In the former case the chief object presented was the perfect acceptance of the sacrifice; in the latter, the judgment due to sin borne by the victim. 3 The chief use of the blood was for atonement The word to make atone- ment, is used in three different senses, namely, to express the covering over of sin, the purging or cleansing the sinner, and the appeasing the wrath of God. The primary sense is to arver over; thus this word is used in Gen. vi. 14, "And thou shalt pitch it within and without with pitch." Here the covering over the ark with a coat of pitch, is expressed by the same word as that which means to atone. How blessed is the thought, as connected with our salvation, that the all-searching eye of God is arrested by the precious blood of Christ, which has so entirely covered over and hidden our sins, that He beholds no iniquity in us! "Blessed is he whose transgression is forgiven, whose sin is covered." 4 (Ps.

xxxii. i.) This is indeed the effectual way in which God blots out transgressions for His own sake and will not remember sins. (Is. xliii. 25.) Again, atonement means also the purging away of sin; thus, in Lev. xvi., one use of the atoning blood of the sin-offerings was to cleanse the holy places from all the uncleanness of the children of Israel (ver. 16-19). * n such cases the blood was always applied to the persons or things to be purged, as, for instance, to the leper and leprous house. (Lev. xiv.) Though we do not read in the law that the Tabernacle and vessels of ministry were sprinkled with blood, yet we are told in Heb. ix. 21, that such was the case; and it was most probably done when the Altar of Burnt-offering was cleansed (Ex. xxix. 36, 37); or it may be that the making atonement for the Altar was looked upon as equivalent to the cleansing with blood the Tabernacle and all the other vessels of ministry, seeing that the Altar was such a leading vessel of service : we find, indeed, a similar action on the great day of atonement, when the cleansing of the Incense Altar was reckoned to be the purging of the holy places of the Tabernacle, and all that was within them. On referring to the following texts, among others, it will be found that the word atonement is translated cleansing or purging 1 Sam. iii. 14; Ps. lxv. 3; lxxix. 9; Is. vi. 7; xxii. 14; xxvii. 9, &c In Heb. ix. there is a blessed contrast drawn between the mere outward purifying, effected under the Mosaic ritual, and the inward purging effected by the precious blood of Christ : " For if the blood of bulls and of goats, and the ashes of an heifer sprinkling the unclean, sanctifieth to the purifying of the flesh; how much more shall the blood of Christ, who through the eternal Spirit offered Himself without spot to God, purge your conscience from dead works to serve the living God ?" (ver. 13, 14). Here the conscience is purged; the Spirit of God applies the blood of Christ to the very seat of defilement, so that the believer has " no more conscience of sins." Not that he loses the consciousness of sin, and its evil movements within, — " If we say that we have no sin, we deceive ourselves, and the truth is not in us" (1 John i. 8), — but it is not allowed to remain defiling the soul, and hindering intercourse with God : when detected it is at once judged and answered by the blood of cleansing, so that it no longer forms a barrier preventing approach to God. The presence of " the living

God " becomes the safe and happy retreat of the purged worshipper; for though he may find even there, that sin is present within him, and that the very fact of being in the light makes manifest the darkness, yet the cleansing power of the blood is known also there in its full and continuous value, and it is ever the witness that sin has been covered over, and every defilement purged away from the heart of the believer. Lastly, the word atonement means the pacifying of wrath. For instance, when Jacob heard that his brother Esau 'was coming, and four hundred men with him, he said, " I will appease him with the present that goeth before me." (Gen. xxxii. 20.) Here the word is the same in the original as atone. The blood of the Lamb has been shed as the only way of appeasing the wrath of God on account of sin; and it becomes the witness that judgment has already been executed on the victim substituted for the sinner. God is now able to "justify by the blood," because He has, in the death of His Son, already judged the sins of many, and His justice has been thereby completely vindicated. Our words propitiation and propitiatory convey the thought of the means by which wrath is appeased, and of the place where mercy has in consequence been established. On the great day of atonement, blood was sprinkled " upon the mercy-seat eastward, and before the mercy-seat." (Lev. xvi. 14.) God's anger against Israel, on account of the sins of the past year, was thereby met, reconciliation was effected, and a way of approach was made into His presence, so that the high priest could stand before the Mercy-seat to consult for the good of the people. To the believer now, the blood of Christ testifies of full and eternal reconciliation : no vengeance on account of sin can break forth against him, for it is the witness that the blessed Lord has borne all wrath and judgment : the way into the Holiest lies open, for the vail has been rent ; and with a blood-sprinkled path into God's presence, a blood-sprinkled Mercy-seat there, and himself with a heart sprinkled from an evil conscience, wherefore need he fear ? why should he pause ? rather let him "draw near with boldness," and taste in fellowship with the Father, and with His Son Jesus Christ, the truth of that message, "God is light, and in Him is no darkness at all."

The all-important truth recorded in Lev. xvii. 11, " It is the blood that maketh atonement for the soul," reiterated in the Epistle to the Hebrews, though with a little difference of expression, "Without shedding of blood is no remission" (Heb. ix. 22), makes our hearts tremble when we think of the unconverted around us. How many trust in vague thoughts of the mercy of God, without at all connecting it with the blood of the Lamb! How many are even offended at the truth respecting the Lord having died as a substitute for sinners under the wrath of God! And may we not turn to some of those who have faith in Jesus, and inquire whether they do really believe that through the shedding of the blood of Christ their sins have been altogether remitted — dismissed from God's remembrance forever? Shall we not find many a heart, even among the children of God, questioning the absolute certainty of this blessed fact as regards themselves, though they may perhaps allow it to be true doctrine in the abstract? This uncertainty and doubtfulness of soul surely arises from the preciousness of that blood not having been pondered over or realized : the example of the Jewish priests of old has not been sufficiently followed ; daily they recurred to the blood of the slain victims, used it in various ways, dipped the finger into it, and sprinkled it according to the prescribed commands, and thus became acquainted with all its varied aspects of cleansing and blessing : the basons for sprinkling at the] Altar were the constant witnesses to them of the uses of the blood. So should it be I with the priests of God now : they should be habituated to the varied and eternal j excellencies of the precious blood of Christ : there ought to be such a realizing of | its value, and understanding of its application and its use, as would answer to the ' dipping of the finger into the bason as of old: constantly there should be a recurrence J to this rich and wondrous provision of God's mercy ; and the soul should be skillful I in this branch of blessed priestly service : " We are come to the blood of sprinkling, that speaketh better things than that of Abel." (Heb. xii. 24.)

When sin had been committed by an Israelite, and had interrupted communion between himself and the Lord, the only way in which intercourse could be restored was through the blood of the sin-

The Holy Vessels and Furniture of the Tabernacle of Israel

offering. (Lev. iv.) If it were a priest that had erred, an offering of the highest value must be sacrificed: . the blood had to be carried in and sprinkled before the vail; the Altar of sweet Incense was also to be touched afresh with it, while all that remained was poured out at the bottom of the Altar of Burnt-offering. This evil was of the deepest character, for it had been committed by one who should have instructed others to avoid it, instead of falling into it himself : as anointed priest, access also into the holy place was his privilege, where he could present incense on the golden altar : this intimate approach to God and this com- munion with Him had been effectually interrupted by sin, so that no fragrance could now ascend from his hands towards the Lord. Blood had therefore to be sprinkled on the place of access, and put on the horns of the Altar, as the only remedy for this defilement, and the only means whereby the forfeited communion could be restored ; while the very foundations, as it were, of the brazen Altar had to be laid afresh in blood. In this case also, the sin-offering was all consumed outside the camp, except a small portion which was burnt upon the Altar of Burnt-offering ; for the fullest appreciation of wrath borne by the victim in behalf of the sinner had to be realized, though, at the same time, the true purity and holiness of the offering itself, and its consequent acceptance by God, were beautifully preserved in the type, by the fact of the innermost portions being burnt as sweetness on the brazen Altar. Herein we have a very complete illustration of the means whereby one, who has previously known fellowship with God, and has wandered into sin, has the soul restored again, so as to be able to renew his forfeited communion. The same truths are indeed for the most part applicable to the first calling and salvation of the sinner out of the world ; but in the instance before us it is rather the restoration of an erring believer that is typified than the first salvation of the sinner. In the case of such an one who has fallen into sin, the soul will have to form a high appreciation of the value of Christ as the sin-offering, in proportion to the greatness of the declension. The worst character of sin is that which may affect or mislead the souls of others. This is pro- bably what is meant by the expression, " If the priest that is anointed do sin accord- ing to the sin of the people" — (Lev. iv. 3), — a sin which might lead the people to transgress, and whereby many might be defiled. Thus, errors in doctrine are more dangerous and contaminating than failures in practical walk.

It is remarkable how little we form our estimates of sin according to this standard. Some gross outrage against morality calls forth strong expressions of reproof ; whereas, a subtle error as to the truth, which may be secretly sapping the very foundations of faith, is too often treated with a morbid charity, which is not really love, but is rather the result of a feeble appreciation of what God most hates. If we compare the First Epistle to the Corinthians with the Epistles to the Galatians and Hebrews, we shall find what a very different estimate of evil the Spirit of God formed, when He severally addressed in the former, persons who were sinning in their moral walk, and in the latter, those who were declining from the truth in doctrine. In the first chapter of the one, Paul speaking by the Spirit says, that God " shall confirm them unto the end blameless in the day of our Lord Jesus Christ " (ver. 8) : in the Galatians he says, " he stands in doubt of them and we know what fearful warnings against irremediable apostasy are given in the sixth and tenth chapters of the Hebrews. The higher the walk of a believer has been with God, and the more influence he has over others, the more deep will his estimate of sin and declension be, if he has failed in his path and looks to the Lord for restoration ; and the more will he love Him who was made sin for us, and value His precious blood as that which cleanseth from all sin, and restores to the soul its full and unhindered power of access even into the Holiest : and not only so, but also enables the soul to present to God that which is of a sweet savour before Him through Jesus Christ. True indeed, the believer is sprinkled with the blood ; no declension or failure can put him back into the state of the unconverted sinner ; he has been once for all sanctified by the will of God through the offering of the body of Jesus Christ, and by that one offering Christ has perfected him forever ; but he will have to recur again and again to the remembrance of that sacrifice, in order to maintain his soul in fellowship with the Father ; and should his conscience be defiled by some known transgression, his only resource will be to retrace again the value of that wondrous* offering for sin, and to weigh the enormity of his own guilt by means of the consuming wrath which has fallen on the head of Jesus in his stead ; he will have to prove more than ever the value of that precious blood which not only has cleansed, but, according to its con- tinued efficacy, " cleanseth us from all sin."

It is instructive to observe the three ways alluded to above in which the blood of the sin-offering was used. First, it was sprinkled " seven times before the Lord, before the vail of the sanctuary." Thus a way of access, which sin had before obstructed, is again made for the priest to draw as near as possible to God : " But now in Christ Jesus, ye who sometimes were far off, are made nigh by the blood of Christ." (Eph. ii. 13.) Next, some of it was put "upon the horns of the Altar of sweet Incense before the Lord." Not only was the place of approach made, but the power to present fragrance of praise and worship was restored. And lastly, "all the blood was poured out at the bottom of the Altar of the Burnt-offering." The basis of acceptance was, as it were, again laid, and the entire remission of sin, and averting of wrath, declared in the pouring out of the blood. 6

"And his flesh-hooks." These instruments were probably used for placing the pieces of the burnt-offering in order on the wood, and for collecting them together as the fire gradually increased, so that they might be perfectly consumed. We find in 1 Sam. ii. 13, 14, a sad misuse of these holy vessels by the sons of Eli. Instead of employing the flesh-hook in the service of the Altar, in order that the sacrifice might be burnt as a sweet savour unto the Lord, they adapted it to their own evil purposes, for ministering to their appetites, turning the holy ordinances of God into a source of gratification of their own lusts. Such the Apostle warns against in Phil. iii. 18, 19 : " For many walk, of whom I have told you often, and now tell you even weeping, that they are the enemies of the cross of Christ ; whose end is destruction, whose god is their belly, and whose glory is in their shame, who mind earthly things." This " turning of the grace of God into lasciviousness" was clearly one of the grievous sins manifested in the house of Eli, and has its parallel at the present day in the merchandize made of the things of

God : the profession of the name of Christ is found to be a source of profit in this world, and the holy truths of God are thus turned into a means of gain, instead of that " godliness with contentment " which is really "great gain." (1 Tim. vi. 6.) " And his fire-pans." These were censers^ as the original word proves, and were attached to the brazen Altar to be used in the court of the Tabernacle ; as those kept at the candlestick, and which were made of gold, were employed in the ministry of the priests inside the Tabernacle. The purpose for which they were made was to contain burning coals taken from off the Altar of Burnt-offering, when incense had to be presented to God ; and probably the fire was transferred into the golden censer from those of brass, when incense was burnt within the holy or most holy place. The fire that consumed the burnt-offering on the final day of the priest's consecration came from God: " And there came a fire out from before the Lord and consumed upon the Altar the Burnt-offering and the fat." (Lev. ix. 24.) God had His own test for that which was presented to Him in sacrifice ; His holiness must be satisfied, and all that was offered to Him must be tried by and yield a sweet savour in full accord- ance with that holiness, if accepted by Him. The searching fire from His presence came forth, and the sweet savour of the victim consumed on the brazen Altar ascended in perfect fragrance towards heaven. No sooner, however, had this blessed token of acceptance been given, than Nadab and Abihu, elated apparently by their high calling as God's priests, "took either of them his censer, and put fire therein, and put incense thereon, and offered strange fire before the Lord which He commanded them not" Again the consuming fire came out from the Lord, and devoured them, and they died before the Lord. Their sin was, that they had not filled their censers with live coals from off the Altar. They disregarded the holiness of God as manifested in the only way in which it could be known, namely, in the fire consuming the victim on the Altar; and they thought to render fragrance acceptable to Him independently of the sacrificial fire. Theirs was a kind of Socinian worship — not a direct denial of God, nor setting aside the incense as if that were not fragrant before the Lord ; but they failed to connect worship with atonement, and thought they could offer a sweet perfume without an immediate link with the Lamb slain. So it is even now ; men may utter the name of Jesus ; they may profess faith in His name, and depict the beauty and sweetness of His character, and admire the truth and holiness of His precepts ; but if the cross is not the ground of all their faith and hope, — if the death of the Lord is not the basis of all their worship, — they present strange fire before the Lord. The sacrifice of Christ tells loudly to the soul of God's judgment. It was by the pre- determinate counsel and foreknowledge of God that Christ was delivered into the hands of sinners to be slain ; He had before showed by the mouth of all His holy pro- phets that Christ should suffer; and the cross is the place where the believer witnesses the judicial hand of God in righteousness, executing vengeance upon sin, at the same time that His holiness has been there fully met and satisfied, and a sweet and blessed savour of acceptance has gone up thence, in which He can rest and delight. And if the fire of the Altar is rejected — if God as the judge is not known in the cross of Christ — the fire of His holiness will descend in devouring vengeance on such hereafter, who thus prove that " they know not God, and obey not the Gospel of our Lord Jesus Christ;" as Nadab and Abihu, who, since they respected not the burning coals of the Altar, had themselves to taste the consuming fire of God's judgment

We have another scene in Israel's history where the brazen censers are mentioned; and again, where judgment is connected with them. In Num. xvi. there is the account of the rebellion of Korah and his company: he endeavoured to usurp a place in the priesthood, though he was not of the family which God had separated off from the tribe of Levi to that office. Two feelings of the flesh seem to have been at work : jealousy respecting the priestly power of Aaron actuated Korah and the Levites who followed him; in the case of those who joined in the conspiracy from the tribe of Reuben, there seems to have been disaffection on account of the kingly power of Moses. The Levites were ambitious of the priestly office — the princes of the congregation disliked the supreme authority of the ruler. Both combined together to assert what in these days would probably be called "their right," in opposition to the appointed order of God. They are accordingly on the morrow tested by the fire of God, and the very attempt to present incense before the Lord calls forth a solemn judgment against them; for they were handling holy things without having been first chosen of God to that service. Korah and his company with the censers had to experience that "God is a consuming fire," because they attempted to draw nigh to Him without having been consecrated for His holy service as priests; while the earth opened and swallowed up those who, though not themselves desiring to intrude into the priest's office, yet made common cause in an act of deep insubjection to God and disobedience of His word. In the case of Nadab and Abihu we have a type of those who, professing to belong to God, disregard the real doctrines of the cross of Christ : in the case of Korah and his company we have a foreshadowing of those who overlook the true qualifications for priesthood. In both cases the judgment of God falls with unabated fury on the adversaries. What solemn warnings may we not gather from hence for our guidance at the present day! We have to watch not only that the true doctrines of the cross are maintained, but also that none be owned as God's priests save those who are born of the priestly family, children of God, and made kings and priests through the blood of the Lamb and the anointing of the Holy Spirit We have steadily to maintain the sovereignty of Christ as lord in His own house. The flesh is as unsubject to the lordship of Christ in the Church as it is to the rule of God in the world. Korah coveted the place of Aaron; Dathan and Abiram disliked the rule of Moses. They united in rebelling against God's order. The whole redeemed Church of God is now the only true priestly family, and alone has title to approach and worship before Him. All the blessed characteristics of the priesthood attach to it ; chosen in Christ before the foundation of the world, and called of God to serve Him, the blood of the Lamb has washed away from it every stain of defilement, and Christ Himself has been made unto it righteousness and true holiness; while the unction and presence of the Holy Ghost is its anointing and living power for service ; and soon the day will come when all false worship and assumptions of men will be judged by the Lord Himself, who "will be revealed from heaven, in flaming fire taking vengeance on them that know not God, and that obey not the Gospel of our Lord Jesus Christ" (2 Thess. i. 7, 8.)

We find the altar derives an additional source of strength from this judgment of God upon Korah; for the direction given is that " The censers of these sinners against their own souls, let them make them broad plates for a covering of the Altar : To be a memorial unto the children of Israel, that no stranger, which is not of the seed of Aaron, come near to offer incense before the Lord ; that he be not as Korah, and as his company." (Num. xvi 38, 40.) Thus, the Altar witnessed from this time forth another additional truth, namely, that there was a distinct priestly family connected with its service, to whom alone belonged the privilege of offering sweet fragrance to God. The broad plates of brass were a solemn memorial of God's judgment against all attempts to gainsay or set aside the order of priesthood He had appointed ; and the very place of sacrifice and acceptance was that also where truths were learnt respecting the family separated off to be the ministers in the sanctuary, and to present sweet incense before Him. Every failure in Israel only the more developed the rich resources of the wisdom and grace of God. The sin of Nadab and Abihu was the occasion for the institution of the great day of atonement (see Lev. xvi. i); the rebellion of Korah was the means of bringing out truth connected with the separated family of God's priests. And thus the more we become conscious of the failings, weaknesses, and sins which daily beset us, and which are widely manifested in the Church of God around, the more should we discover the rich and abundant resources of grace stored up for the saints of God in the Lord Jesus, and the wondrous and varied adaptation of His sacrifice and priesthood to meet our every need, and to cover our every failure. As the altar, with its additional covering of brass, was a constant witness to Israel respecting the title alone of the house of Aaron to come near and offer incense before the Lord, so the sacrifice of Christ, learnt under the teaching of our great High Priest Himself, instructs us as to the family of God which is separated off from the world, " to offer up spiritual sacrifices acceptable to God by Jesus Christ," and "to shew forth the praises of Him who hath called us out of darkness into His marvellous light."

This sixteenth chapter of Numbers introduces again at the close the censer with its holy fire. The plague had broken out among the people, for their murmuring hearts had caught the infection of Koran's sin : " And Moses said unto Aaron, Take a censer, and put fire therein from off the altar, and put on incense, and go quickly unto the congregation, and make an atonement for them ; for there is wrath gone out from the Lord ; the plague is begun. And Aaron took as Moses commanded, and ran into the midst of the congregation; and, behold, the plague was begun among the people: and he put on incense, and made an atonement for the people. And he stood between the dead and the living; and the plague was stayed." (ver, 46-48.) The censer was now in the hands of no " stranger," but of him who had just title to use it ; the fire was also no " strange fire," but was from the altar where it had fed upon the slain lamb ; and a cloud of sweet perfume ascended towards God, covering over the ill-savour of the murmurings and rebellions of Israel, and forming a line of safety separating off the living from the dead. No plague, no destroying vengeance, could pass that fragrant barrier ; for the testimony it gave forth was of holiness met and satisfied in the death of the sacrifice : on the one side lay the thousands slain in judgment ; on the other stood the saved hosts of the Lord. What a beautiful type does this give us of the safety of those who are sheltered under the sweet savour of the Lamb slain, recorded on their behalf before God by the living High Priest! Children of wrath by nature, even as others, they are saved solely through the atoning virtue of that death, ministered by the living power of the Priest who is able " to save to the uttermost those that come unto God by Him." While death and judgment steadily pursue their course on the one hand, life and salvation is the eternal portion of those who are under the blessed shelter of the Lord. No destruc- tive wrath can intrude among those thus protected; but outside that favoured band vengeance and death triumph with unrestrained fury. There is a memorable precept respecting this Altar recorded in Lev. vi. 9, 12, 13, which is designated "the law of the burnt-offering : it is the burnt-offering, because of the burning upon the altar all night unto the morning, and the fire of the altar shall be burning in it The fire upon the altar shall be burning in it ; it shall not be put out : and the priest shall burn wood on it every morning, and lay the burnt-offering in order upon it; and he shall burn thereon the fat of the peace-offerings. The fire shall ever be burning upon the altar: it shall never go out." Thus, a constant memorial of sacrifice was to be kept before the Lord, and also a vessel ever ready for the worship of Israel. During the night until the morning, especially, the odour of a sweet savour was to ascend to the Lord from the burnt-offering; for the night was the time of Israel's most entire helplessness, and when the powers of darkness might be most abroad to molest them ; but the word of the Lord had provided the fragrance of the ascending sacrifice, which would effectually retain the presence and power of God in the midst of them for their defence and protection. Whether buried in the unconsciousness of sleep, or busied with the many needful activities of life, still the memorial of His mercy in the death of the lamb was ever before Him : though they might forget awhile what holy God tabernacled among them, He had provided a remembrance of them in the lamb slain, which should be ever fragrant Truly may we say, the sweet savour of the death of Christ, perpetuated through the ceaseless ministry of our High Priest, is ever our memorial of acceptance with God : sheltered under that, no ill-savour of ours can awaken wrath — no accusation of the enemy can prevail. Again, and again did the adversary seek to bring down a curse upon Israel, when Balaam was hired to do the evil work. But, encamped in beautiful order, " like trees of lign-aloes which the Lord had planted" around the Tabernacle of God, where the ceaseless sweet savour of the burnt-offering covered over every defilement, what accusations could avail ? what enemy could triumph? God looked out upon His hosts from off the Mercy-seat, and He beheld them under the shelter of the cloud of incense and the sweet savour of the lamb slain, when Satan sought to accuse them and have them cursed. All their murmurings and rebellions were forgotten; all their sins and iniquities were remembered no more ; He had blessed, and none could reverse it ; " He had not beheld | iniquity in Jacob, neither had he seen perverseness in Israel." «The forty years of provocation were forgotten, for the odour of the sacrifice filled the heart and thoughts of Jehovah.

One other thought may be suggested respecting this Altar, and which indeed is true in principle respecting all the worship at the Tabernacle, namely, that all minis- trations connected with it had reference to the whole nation, even if they more immediately concerned some private individuals of that nation. The Altar had ever a corporate aspect: no person was allowed to have a private altar of his own; but if he would draw nigh to God, it must be where the worship of the whole people was conducted. Thus, the Tabernacle, with its holy vessels, served as a bond of union, drawing the people together, and linking them closely one with another. Sprung from one source, and belonging to one God, Israel had ever in its worship the memorial of that unity." The Church of God now has not only a unity but a union; not only are those who compose it sprung from one heavenly source, but there is an indissoluble union of life subsisting, as between the body and its members, and that life is in the Son. Every exercise therefore of that life, even in each individual, affects the whole body, though in a remote degree, and often unappreciated by us. If Israel of old were gathered round the Tabernacle, and learnt again and again there to estimate its unity as one people, serving one and the same God, much more have the saints of God now to remember, in all their worship and service, that they are united to Christ, and consequently are members one of another. There cannot be such a thing as an isolated Christian. The very presence of the Holy Ghost forbids it; "for by one Spirit have we been all baptized into one body;" and the cross itself is the witness that Christ "loved the Church and gave Himself for it." The Apostle in the Epistle to the Ephesians, while earnestly praying that those to whom he wrote might be able to comprehend "what is the breadth, and length, and depth, and height, and to know the love of Christ, which passeth knowledge," yet inserts the words, "with all saints " so impossible would it be to comprehend even the love of the Lord Himself, unless the soul were conscious of the union that subsists between all the redeemed family of God. We may here close for a while our meditations on this wide field of blessed truth. It has in reality but just been entered upon; for it is a boundless subject, seeing it treats of the wisdom and grace of God in the gift of His Son, and of the love of Christ which passeth knowledge. Enough, however, may have been written to interest the souls of some of the Lord's people, and induce them to search more deeply into the mine of blessed instruction which the types present.

NOTES TO THE ALTAR OF BURNT-OFFERING.

Our translation seldom makes any distinction between the words Tabernacle and Tent, though In the original they are never confounded. The word Tabernacle, or dwelling, is the name appropriated to the holy building and its precincts, when it is regarded especially as the residence of God. It was His dwelling-place — His Tabernacle. On the other hand, the word tent is always used when reference is made to the congregation; so that it is never called the Tabernacle of the congregation, but always the tent of the congregation. God's dwelling-place was the tent where they assembled: they did not dwell there, but there they congregated and met God. In the following texts both terms are used, the Tabernacle, and the tent of the congregation. (Ex. xxxix. 32, 40;xl. 2, 29, 34, 35.) a There is a difficulty, acknowledged by all, in understanding the phrase translated: "And thou shalt put it under the compass of the altar beneath." The word "compass" 2313, found nowhere else in the Bible, is supposed by Gesenius to mean, "a circuit or border which went round the middle of the Altar, over the brazen grating ; perhaps in order to catch whatever might fall from the Altar." It is difficult to know what he means by this. The Septuagint evidently mistakes the passage altogether in Ex. xxvii. ; and in Ex. xxxviii. this word seems to be translated by TrapdOifia, an appendage, and there the grate is confounded with this appendage. Whatever may be the true meaning, it seems plain from all the context, that the grate was placed inside the Altar, half-way up ; and it is remarkable that it would thus reach just to the same height as the top of the Ark. The Mercy-seat and the sacrificial victim would be presented before God on the same level. The following is a summary of the various ways in which the blood of the principal sacrifices was used : — The blood of the burnt-offerings, peace-sacrifices, ram of consecration, and trespass-offerings, was sprinkled, pit, on the Altar of Burnt - offering round about. (Lev. i. 5, 11 ; iii. 2, 8, 13 ; xvii. 6 ; ix. 18 ; vii. 14 ; viii. 24 ; vii. 2.)

THE ALTAR OF BURNT- OFFERING.

The blood of the sin-offerings was never sprinkled round about upon the Altar. It was sprinkled, before the vail (Lev. iv. 6, 17); upon the Mercy-seat eastward, and before the Mercy-seat (Lev. xvi. 14, 15) ; on the Incense Altar (Lev. xvi. 19) ; on Aaron and his sons, and their garments. (Lev. viii. 30.) In all these cases of sprinkling the blood of the sin-offerings, the finger was used. The blood of sin-offerings was also put with the finger on the horns of the Incense Altar (Lev. iv. 7, 18); or on the horns of the Altar of Burnt-offering. (Lev. iv. 25, 30, 34; viii. 15 ; ix. 9.) The blood of sin-offerings only was poured out at the bottom of the Brazen Altar. (Lev. iv. 7 § 18, 25, 30, 34; viii. 15; ix. 9.)

This aspect of the blood of atonement was thoroughly realized, and touch ingly expressed by the "happy mute," who was instructed by Charlotte Elizabeth. He said "that Jesus Christ had passed His red hand over the page of sin, in the book of God's remembrance, and had left nothing visible there but the blood which had flowed from His palm, when pierced by the nails on Calvary.' Blood was poured out as a token of sin remitted, and of judgment averted. "Without shedding of blood is no remission." (Heb. ix. 22.) And "Moses kept the passover, and the pouring forth of blood, lest he that destroyed the first-born should touch them." (Heb. xi. 28 ; here the word is irp6ox vai C-)

The Holy Vessels and Furniture of the Tabernacle of Israel

The Holy Vessels and Furniture of the Tabernacle of Israel

H.W. Soltau

www.ingramcontent.com/pod-product-compliance
Lightning Source LLC
Chambersburg PA
CBHW050319120526
44592CB00014B/1975